braidmaking

TMA

This book belongs
to Thérèse Anton
February 1992

braidmaking

Barbara Pegg

A & C Black · London

First published 1990 by A & C Black (Publishers) Ltd
35 Bedford Row, London WC1R 4JH

Photographs by John Simmons

A CIP catalogue record for this book is available from the British Library.

Filmset in 10/12 Photina by August Filmsetting, Haydock, St Helens

Printed in Great Britain by
Whitstable Litho Printers Ltd., Whitstable, Kent.

ISBN 0 7136 31988

Contents

Colour plates after 16, 32, 48 and 64

Introduction

Braids are a particular aspect of textiles which have fascinated me for a number of years, probably because beautiful textiles which have been made by hand with virtually no special equipment hold a special interest for me. Braidmaking seems to exemplify how much can be made with so little and the end results are so intricate and cleverly constructed that we can only marvel at how our craftmaking predecessors invented these techniques.

As a craftswoman, teacher and writer on textile crafts, I have always been keen to discover how textiles are made and to learn about their history and origins, and I gradually developed the idea of compiling a range of braidmaking techniques in one book which could be attractive and useful as a resource for anyone interested in textiles and related crafts.

In *Braidmaking* I have described a braid as a narrow textile of hand-manipulated construction which can be made using various techniques such as plaiting, knotting, looping and weaving. The last is sometimes said not strictly to be a braidmaking technique, as it uses two separate sets of threads, warp and weft, but I have included it, since so many narrow textile braids have been devised by weavers in different cultures throughout history that I felt it was an important part of the development of braidmaking and shouldn't be left out. There are also, no doubt, a number of other braidmaking methods which I haven't included and which even now I'm discovering, so this is only the tip of the iceberg!

There is some confusion between the terms 'braiding' and 'plaiting' and the two words seem to have become interchangeable descriptions for one technique. I have, therefore, used braidmaking as an overall description for all the techniques in the book, and plaiting as the method of making narrow braids from threads which interlace or interlink in a diagonal direction.

Textile technique may be divided into two main types:

1 Those produced with one 'thread', that is netting, lace, knitting and crochet
   (a) with a 'limited' thread, where the end of the thread is drawn through a previous loop, as in netting and lace;
   (b) with an 'endless' thread; that part of the thread nearest to the last loop is pulled through, as in knitting and crochet.

2 Those produced with two or more sets of threads, that is plaiting, macramé and weaving.

The 'threads' may be any pliable material: wool, cotton, linen, silk, nylon, cane, raffia, etc.

I have attempted to define the four main sections of *Braidmaking* as follows:

Plaiting

Separate threads interlacing or interlinking on a diagonal path in a systematic way to make a flat, round, square, convex or concave braid.

Knotted braids

Threads looping round and through one another and pulled into knots, either in one continuous thread as in finger knotting, or with several separate threads, as in macramé.

Looped braids

Made from a continuous thread which is turned back on itself to form a loop through which another part or the end of the thread may pass, as in knitting, netting and crochet.

Woven braids

Separate threads acting as warp and/or weft:
(a) where both are interchangeable, as in finger weaving;
(b) where they are two separate elements, as in backstrap and tablet weaving.

The final chapter, 'Fringes and tassels', suggests ways in which these techniques can be used and combined to make decorative finishes.

Braids are not only fascinating to make in themselves but, combined with other crafts such as weaving, embroidery, patchwork, knitting and many kinds of stitchcraft, they can add an extra dimension to your work. Many exciting innovations are being made in contemporary textile crafts with mixed techniques and materials. I hope that *Braidmaking* will enable you to discover new ideas for the textiles you are making today from the techniques we have learned from the past.

Plaiting

Plaiting is a technique in which a set of threads are interlaced or woven through one another to make a narrow braid. In order to do this, the complete set is divided into two elements so that in any one row one thread, or group of threads, is taken over and under the rest to make the structure. Plaiting appears to be closely related to weaving but differs in that the two elements are interchangeable so that, whereas in weaving there are warp and weft threads which are separate groups, in plaiting any one thread, or threads, can act either as warp or weft in a row, and their roles can change in another row. The other particularly recognizable feature of plaiting is that the threads interlace obliquely, so all plaited braids have a distinctly diagonal emphasis.

The simplest plaits, made with loose, unattached threads, can be worked with a minumum of three threads, or three groups, up to greater numbers of threads to make wider, more intricate braids, so the plaits in the first part of this chapter get their names from the number of threads they use, for example the eight-strand cross-over plait or the twelve-strand twill braid. Once you are fully familiar with the three-strand plait, you will then understand the concept of plaiting when worked with more threads.

In this chapter I have also included Indian finger braids, often called 'finger weaving'. Half-way between a plait and a weave, Indian braids offer a lot of scope for making colourful, patterned sashes and wider braids. Finally there is a section on sprang, also a plaiting technique but worked quite differently. The threads are stretched inside a frame and each one is interlinked diagonally with the adjoining thread to make a netlike structure, or, as with the Hopi wedding sash, interlaced obliquely to the selvedges.

In all these plaiting methods it is the feature of the threads having a diagonal emphasis which identifies them and gives them their attractive patterning. You can choose from a wide range of materials for plaited braids: matt and shiny cotton threads, yarns of different types and thicknesses whether textured or tightly spun, silks, linens and synthetic yarns. For your first samples, smooth cotton or yarn will enable you to see the structural form and pattern closely, and with sprang a strong thread is advisable to withstand the tension it is held in. The use of colour is very important as plaited braids can show their patterning to better effect if contrasting and complementary colours are used.

Plait made with the twining technique, see p. 21.

PLAITING WHERE THE ENDS OF THREADS ARE NOT FIXED

This first section is about plaiting with loose threads. All kinds of threads can be used attractively, combining colour and texture. The black-and-white illustrations show samples made in dark and light cotton twine, but in nearly every plait, the combination of dark and light or coloured threads could be changed to give a different finished effect. For the length of your threads, allow half as much again as the finished length of plait you require.

You will find plaiting easier if you work on a board or cushion using pins to hold the threads in place. See p. 41 for how to set this up. The ends of the threads can be secured at the top temporarily with an overhand knot or with a twined thread, leaving a fringe allowance (Diag. 1). The top of the group of threads is then pinned to your board and you plait downwards to the length you want, easing the threads close together as you work so that the finished plait, whether flat or round, is firm. You can apply plaits as decorative braids to furnishings and fabrics with stitching or for wearable sashes or decorative hanging plaits. Finish the ends with plaited, knotted or wrapped fringes and tassels, see p. 70.

Three-strand plait
This is the simplest plait which most of us learned as children. The over–under progression of the threads makes a simple structure which is characteristic of plaiting. Tie an overhand knot in three threads and pin them to a piece of soft board or a firm cushion. The threads are numbered 1–3, left to right, and 3 starts by moving over 2 and under 1. Then 2 moves over 1 and under 3. Finally 1 moves over 3 and under 2, till the threads are back in their original order (Diag. 2). This sequence is repeated to make a flat plait and can be made with more threads arranged in groups of three for a thicker or a multicoloured braid.

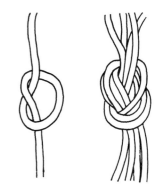

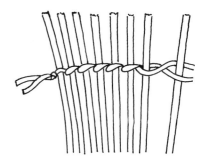

Diagram 1

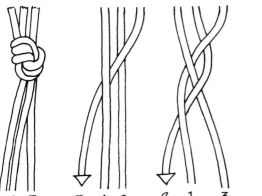
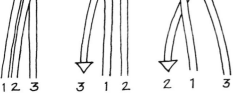

1 2 3   3 1 2   2 1 3   1 2 3

Diagram 2

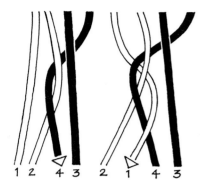

Four-strand plait

This round plait, or cord, is made with four threads, and the pattern of the structure shows very clearly when two pairs of different colours are used. Tie an overhand knot in two light and two dark threads, and pin them to a board so that the light threads are on the left and the dark threads on the right. Take the right thread under two to the left and back over one to the right. Now take the left thread under two to the right and back over one to the left (Diag. 3). These two steps repeated make a cord as shown in the photo on p. 11. Pull the threads fairly taut and hold them slightly away from the board as you work. A different arrangement of colours was used for another cord in the photo on p. 11, with two dark threads either side of two light threads in the centre, but the plaiting sequence was the same.

Five-strand plait

It looks very like the three-strand, but is firmer because of the extra strands and is just as quick to do. It is made in two steps which are repeated. First the far right thread is taken over the next two threads to the centre, then the far left thread comes over the two next to it, to the centre (Diag. 4). After five steps the order of the threads is reversed and after ten they are all back in their original positions.

Diagram 3

Diagram 4

Six-strand plait (round)

This is a firm round braid and is attractive when made in two colours. If you arrange three light threads on the left and three dark on the right, the pattern of the braid will emerge as alternate vertical stripes, see photograph below. The pattern sequence for making this plait and its final appearance are similar to the four-strand plait with the threads arranged light on the left and dark on the right. Here though the braid is thicker with more stripes.

Start on the left with thread 1, take it under 2, 3, 4 and 5 to the right, then turn back to the left and take it over 5 and under 4. On the right take thread 6 under 5, 4, 1 and 3, and then turn it back to the right over 3 and under 1. These two steps are repeated, taking the outermost left thread under four threads, then over one and under one back to the left, and the same sequence with the far right thread (Diag. 5). Take care to keep the threads in their correct order as you work and not to twist them or the pattern will alter. You will find as you plait this braid that after each step the two colours always remain grouped together, light on the left, dark on the right. You can of course try other arrangements of colours for different patterns.

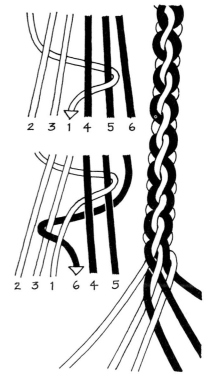

Diagram 5

The plaits shown left to right are made with: (*1*) 3 strands (*2*) Two with 4 strands (*3*) 5 strands (*4*) 6 strands, round (*5*) 6 strands, flat.

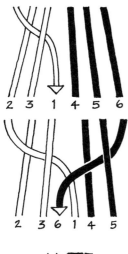

Diagram 6

Six-strand plait (flat)

A diagonal striped pattern is made with this plait if the threads are arranged three light on the left and three dark on the right. Begin with the left thread 1 and take it over 2 and under 3. Then pick up right thread 6 and take it under 5 and over 4 and 1. Continue with these two steps, taking the far left thread each time over one and under one thread to the centre, then bringing the far right thread under one and over two threads to the centre (Diag. 6).

Eight-strand plaits

There seem to be quite a variety of eight-strand plaits; here are five quite different ones.

Square plaited braid

A striking four-faceted braid, this is made in a similar way to the four-strand plait with two steps which are repeated. Arrange four light threads on the left and four dark threads on the right. Take the far right thread and pass it under five threads towards the left, then back over two to the right.

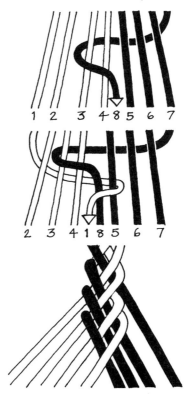

Diagram 7

In the same way, take the far left thread and pass it under five threads towards the right, then back over two to the left (Diag. 7). The two groups, light and dark, will always stay in their left and right positions after each step and the resulting braid is vertically striped alternately in dark and light. By arranging the threads differently, various patterns can be made in the braid, for example, a chevron pattern is created by alternating dark and light threads.

Cross-over plait

This is a broad, flat plait in which the threads curve gracefully down the braid. Arrange three light threads on the right and left with two dark threads in the centre. Begin with the right of centre dark thread and take it under the other dark thread and over the three light threads to the left. Then take the left of centre dark thread under the three light threads to the right. Pick up the three left light threads and, keeping them parallel with one another, cross them over the right three threads. Bring the far left dark thread under the left group of light threads to the centre, and bring the far right dark thread over the right light threads to the centre. These three steps are repeated (Diag. 8).

Chinese plait

This plait is made in two steps which are repeated and is very quick and easy to do. Arrange the threads so there are three dark, two light and three dark. Start with the far left thread and take it over two dark and a light thread to the centre. Then take the far right thread over two dark, a light and the dark thread now being at the centre (Diag. 9). As you repeat this sequence a dramatic chevron pattern emerges.

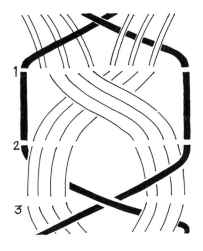

Diagram 8

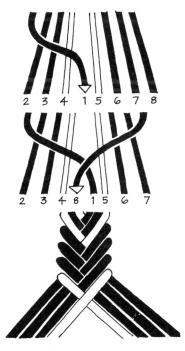

Diagram 9

The five plaits shown here are all made with 8 strands. Left to right: (*1*) square plait (*2*) Cross-over plait (*3*) Chinese plait (*4*) Alternating plait (*5*) Twisted plait.

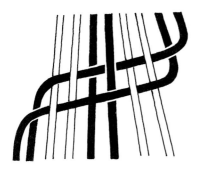

Diagram 10

In these two eight-strand plaits, the threads are interlaced through one another in an under and over sequence, like the weft through the warp in plain weaving. It is especially important with these braids to keep the threads in their correct order, so a board to work on, with pins, is essential.

Eight-strand alternating plait

Arrange the threads so that you have two dark, two light, two dark and two light, right to left. Start with the far right dark thread and weave it over, then under, each of the threads in turn. Then take the next right dark thread and weave it over, then under, each of the threads, including the last thread which you were weaving with in the previous row (Diag. 10). With each successive thread from the right becoming a weft thread on each row, you will pass it over and under what was under and over on the row before. Adjust the tension as you work by easing the threads close to one another so that the downwards threads emphasize the diagonal dark and light stripes in the plait.

This plait could be made in four different colours for a really colourful striped braid.

Eight-strand twisted plait

This braid is not entirely flat when finished but begins to have the convex/ concave surface which is even more of a feature in the following two plaits. The slight twist appears down either edge of the braid, created by the outer left and right threads on each row as they move in towards the centre.

Start with the far left thread and weave it over one, under two and over one to the centre. Then weave the far right thread under one, over two and under one to the centre (Diag. 11). Repeat this row, taking great care to keep the threads in their correct order. It is easy to confuse threads in this braid because it is quite a while before you can see the pattern and structure emerging clearly.

After each row, adjust the tension by grasping the left and the right group of four threads and pulling them firmly, so that you ease the threads close together. With the arrangement of threads illustrated here, the dark and light groups will move diagonally across the braid to the opposite edge, then back again, so that in every eighth row they will be back in their original places.

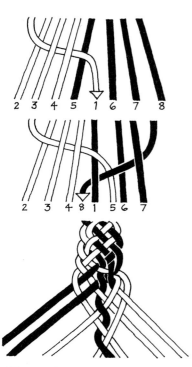

Diagram 11

Nine-strand or double plait

This is a chevron-patterned braid with a very unusual structure, where one face of the braid is convex and the other is concave. The threads are arranged as follows: two dark, two light, one dark, two light and two dark. Take the far left dark thread under two and over two to the centre. Then take the far right dark thread under two and over two towards the centre (Diag. 12). Repeat these two steps and after every few rows pull the threads firmly to keep them evenly tensioned.

This plait can also be made with seven threads arranged dark and light alternately. The first step is the same as for the nine-strand plait. For the second step, take the far right thread over two threads towards the centre.

Eleven-strand plait

This plait also has a convex/concave structure, but more pronounced than the seven or nine-strand plaits. Arrange the threads so that you have six dark on the left and five light on the right. First weave the far left dark thread under two and over three to the centre. Then take the far right light thread under two and over three to the centre (Diag. 13). Continue weaving the left and the right threads to the centre in this way. Keep a firm hold on the tension of the threads after two or three rows to keep the plaiting even. The photograph below shows the plait from the convex side.

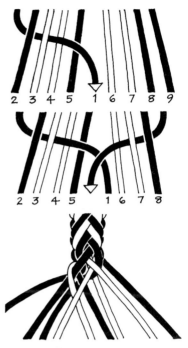

Diagram 12

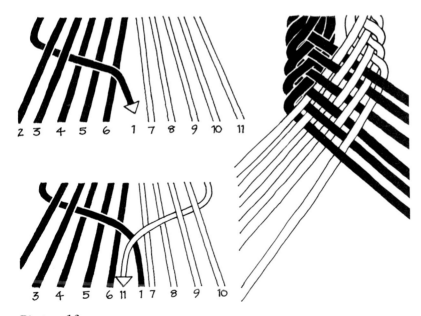

Diagram 13

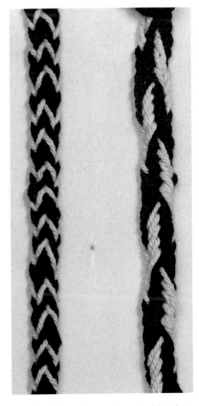

On the left, a 9-strand or double plait, and on the right, an 11-strand plait.

Diagram 14

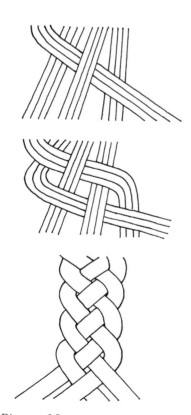

Diagram 15

Twelve-strand 2/2 twill braid

Twill is a weave structure which differs from over one, under one plain weave. An even twill can be made with the weft passing under two, over two warp threads, or under three, over three, and is usually written as 2/2 or 3/3, the first number being the number of warp threads the weft passes under, and the second the number of warp threads it passes over. The result is an equal balance in the structure of the warp and weft. There are also uneven twills, for example, under three and over one thread, 3/1, will give a weave structure with two different faces, with warp floats showing on one face and weft floats on the reverse.

In this 2/2 even-twill braid, begin with the far left thread and weave it under two and over two across all the threads. Repeat with the next thread now on the far left, and continue in the same way with further rows (Diag. 14). Use pins to hold the threads and adjust the tension so that the braid is firm with straight edges. You will see that the threads are equally balanced with those threads that are acting as warp running down the braid, under two and over two, whilst the threads acting as wefts move obliquely across the braid, under two and over two.

Left, a 12-strand 2/2 twill braid, and on the right, a 12-strand cross-over plait.

Colour plate: Making braids requires little equipment. Some pieces of wood, tablets, and a selection of yarns are all you need to start.

Twelve-strand cross-over plait

This is another gracefully curving braid like the eight-strand plait. It is made with four groups of three threads which interlace over and under one another. The threads must be kept flat and parallel throughout, so you may find it easier to keep them flat at the beginning if you twine across them with a finer thread, about 15 cm (6 in.) from the cut ends of the threads at the top (Diag. 1, p. 9).

Begin with the far left group of three threads and take them over, under and over the other three groups. Repeat with the next group now on the far left (Diag. 15). Keep weaving the threads acoss in this way, and adjust the tension and spacing so that all the threads are evenly grouped. Using a board and pins will help you a great deal.

Indian finger braids

Indian finger braiding, often called finger weaving, is a very old method of interlacing threads into narrow bands, so called because the fingers of the braider are the only equipment needed to manipulate the threads.

People in many parts of the world have used similar techniques to make belts and sashes to wear, as well as straps for tying and carrying everyday items. In addition to utilitarian braids, crafts people developed others which combined great skill and beauty for special occasions such as weddings, festivals and as a feature of ceremonial costume.

The technique itself is really a half-way stage between plaiting and weaving. The weft is woven through the warp in successive rows but, where the two elements are separate and distinct in other forms of weaving, here their roles are interchangeable. For this reason, and also because the weft travels diagonally through the warp, a distinct feature of plaiting, I have included finger braids in this chapter. As you will see, when you try this technique, these plaits are quite a development from those described earlier and, although they are more intricate and take longer to complete, the end results are well worth the effort.

The method used in finger braids can be described in the following way. One thread, acting as a weft, is taken over and under other threads, acting as the warp, to make a row of weaving. As each row changes, so the threads which are acting as warp and weft change. The patterns come about through the colour arrangement of the threads at the beginning and the sequence in which they are woven. Some of the most highly developed finger braids came from the Indians of Ancient Peru nearly two thousand years ago, and from North American Indian tribes, so I have limited the examples described here to some of their techniques.

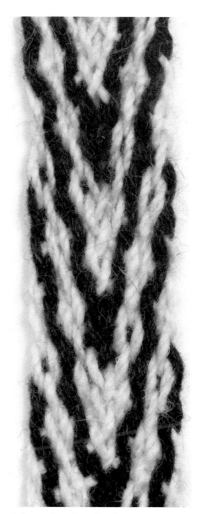

A finger braid in the Peruvian chevron pattern, see p. 19.

Colour plate: Plaited braids, l to r: (1) 5-strands, (2) 12-strand cross-over, (3) Indian finger braid, (4) 8-strand Chinese, (5) 8-strand square, (6) 11-strand, and (7) 8-strand cross-over.

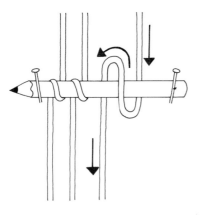

Diagram 16

Setting up the threads

You will first need to estimate the length of braid you want to make, allowing between 15–20 cm (6–8 in.) for fringes at each end. Cut the threads $1\frac{1}{2}$ times the finished length to allow for take up during the weaving. It's probably best to try a short length as a sample for learning a particular technique. The number of threads you will need will depend on which braid you choose to make, and how wide you want it to be.

The middle of each thread is looped around a pencil (Diag. 16) in the correct order for the pattern. You will then weave from the middle first to one end, then to the other, so your pattern will be centred on the braid. To enable you to braid more easily, tie an overhand knot in all the threads above the pencil and pin the knot to a board. Secure the pencil to the board with pins above and below it (Diags. 17 and 18).

Weaving the braids

Weaving is begun just below the pencil and consists of making a shed in the warp threads by picking up alternate threads so that you can pass a weft thread through it, and on the following and succeeding rows, picking up the opposite warp threads so that another weft can be passed through. How you manipulate the threads with your fingers will depend on the type of braid you are making and the number of threads you are handling, but here are a few tips which might help.

It can help if you tension the warp threads by trapping them under a bulldog clip attached to the bottom of the board (the weft thread on each row is left loose). You can then use your fingers to make the shed in the warp and to pass the weft through. After each row, undo the clip, tighten the weft and drop it down with the other threads. If you have a lot of fine threads, you may find it easier to make the shed using a knitting needle or thin stick rather than your fingers. Use pins to keep the threads in place, and the edges straight, particularly with diagonal patterned braids, which distort easily. Weave a few rows loosely, then adjust the tension and ease the warp threads closely together. When you have woven the first half, turn the board around, untie the knot and remove the pencil. Pull out the loops, straighten the threads and weave the second half of the braid in the same way as the first. To finish the fringes, see p. 70 for different ideas.

Finally, block the braid flat on an ironing board with pins, and lightly steam-press it.

Peruvian braid with a diagonal stripe

This simple braid was probably one of the earliest methods of finger braiding used by the weavers of Ancient Peru. Weaving is shown here from left to right, with the far left thread acting as the weft in each row (Diag. 17). (You can weave from right to left if you prefer.) The diagonal striped pattern is emphasized best if you pull the warp threads closely together so that the weft doesn't show, and you get a dense braid. Arrange at least two threads of the same colour together on the pencil to get a stripe, and try varying the widths of the stripes (photograph facing p. 32).

Chevron

This pattern is made by weaving the threads from the centre to the edges. The braid in the photograph on p. 17 was made in blue and cream yarn, with the threads arranged in the following way: 3C/2B/3C/4B/3C/2B/3C. Note the threads are arranged symmetrically from the centre.

Start below the pencil with the right-of-centre blue thread and weave it over and under each thread to the left edge. Then take the left-of-centre blue thread and weave it over and under each thread to the right edge. Continue in this way and after a few rows, ease the warp threads closely together (Diag. 18).

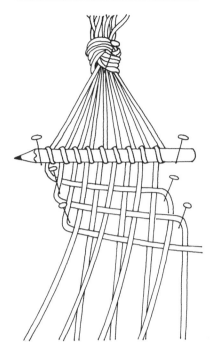

Diagram 17

Peruvian repp braids

The weavers of Ancient Peru devised certain methods of finger braids which were unique and this is not so surprising when we know that their textiles reached a high level of skill and sophistication. One particular technique known as repp was to weave grouped wefts through single warp threads and vice versa, which meant that braids could be made where some of the coloured threads could cover others, to be later uncovered again. The resulting patterns, which could be complex and quite distinct, do not seem to have been discovered in finger braids found elsewhere (photograph on p. 20).

The braid shown in the photograph on p. 20 was woven with grouped wefts through single warps, followed by single wefts through grouped warp threads. The threads are arranged in the following order: 4A/4B/4C/8B/4C/4B/4A and, when you have tried this first sample, you can then experiment with colour arrangements and patterns by varying the use of the grouped threads to design your own patterns.

Start below the pencil with the left group of four A threads and weave them as one weft over and under single warp threads to the centre. Weave the right group of A threads in the same way and cross the groups at the centre by weaving the right group through a shed in the left group; make another three rows in the same way on the left and the right with threads B, C and B, so that the threads are back in their original positions.

Start now with the first single A thread on the left and weave it over the rest of the A threads, then under and over the other warp threads, having arranged them in groups of four, to the centre. Weave the right single A thread in the same way and cross the threads at the centre. Keeping the wefts loosely woven, make another three rows on the left and right with the other three single A threads, weaving them through grouped warp threads. Ease the wefts closely together, so that at this stage in the first four

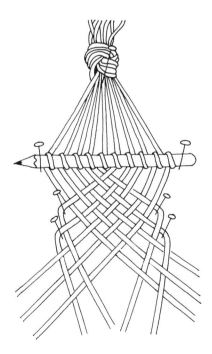

Diagram 18

A finger braid using the Peruvian repp technique, see p. 19.

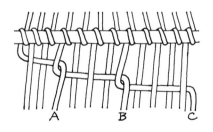

Diagram 19

rows the warp threads completely cover the wefts, and in the second four rows the wefts cover the warp threads.

The pattern throughout the braid is made by repeating the eight rows as described above, always starting with the outermost left and right threads and weaving them to the centre.

American Indian lightning pattern

Dramatic zig-zag patterns often occur in American Indian textiles, whether in blankets, rugs or sashes. This braid design uses an interlocking technique to create a lightning pattern which is unique and very striking. The photograph facing p. 32 shows a cotton braid with the threads arranged in the following way: 8A/8B/8C. The threads are woven from left to right, and each row consists of three stages.

1 Take the far left A thread under the next left thread, then over and under until you reach the fourth B thread. Interlock the A with the B thread (Diag. 19), drop the A thread alongside the remaining threads and continue weaving with the B thread.
2 Take the B thread over the next B thread, then under and over each thread until you reach the fourth C thread. Interlock the B with the C thread, drop the B thread alongside the others and continue weaving with the C thread.

3 Take the C thread over the next C thread, then under, over and under the last C threads to complete the row.

This technique of weaving and interlocking is repeated in each row; in the second row, however, the left A thread weaves up to and interlocks with the third B thread, which in turn does the same with the third C thread. In the third row, interlocking takes place with the second B and C threads, and in the fourth row, with the first B and C threads. At the end of the fourth row, all the threads are back in their original positions. The four pattern rows are then repeated continuously.

The tension should be kept fairly loose in the first four rows but after they are completed, ease the threads closer together and adjust the tension of the interlocked threads. You can adjust the threads more easily in subsequent rows as the correct tension becomes apparent.

You may also want to push a pin through each interlock into the board as you weave each row, to hold the threads in place until the next row is completed. After every four rows remove the pins, and adjust the tension.

To weave the other half of the braid, turn it around and remove the pencil as described on p. 18. Pin the threads to the board and continue to weave from left to right, but the colours will now be in reverse order, 8C, 8B and 8A, so you will start each row with the far left C thread, interlock it with a B thread, then take a B thread and interlock with an A thread.

Double-lightning patterns can be made with larger numbers of threads. For example 8A/8B/10C/8B/8A (Diag. 20). You make the first row with the left of centre C thread to the right edge, weaving and interlocking fourth threads as described already, then with the right of centre C thread weaving and interlocking to the left edge. Subsequent rows interlock third, second and first threads, and then the pattern is repeated again.

Twined plaiting

This is another finger plait used by the Peruvians to make braids. Here, though, the threads aren't woven through one another but are twined around one another in pairs. You will find this more intricate to do than the others, but well worth the effort. Mount the threads on a pencil as already described. The total must be an even number as they are worked in pairs. The braid in the photograph facing p. 32 was made in three colours, arranged as follows: 6A/8B/6C. For your first twined plait, use a smooth cotton, then the threads won't tangle so much as wool, and keep the left and right groups apart, except when joining at the centre.

Make the first twining row with the far left pair of A threads. Start by passing one thread behind and one in front of the second pair. Twist the two A threads away from you so that they change places. Pass one thread in front and one behind the third pair. Twist them away from you again. Continue in this way, twisting the twining pair in the spaces between the other pairs so that you encircle them, until you reach the centre. Keep the twining pair separate.

Now twine with the far right pair of threads to the centre, again twisting away from you (Diag. 21a). Twist each of the twining pairs once more, then interweave them as shown in Diag. 21b. The next row of twining is made first from the left, then the right, except that the pairs of twining threads are twisted towards you, so that the angle of twining lies in the opposite direction to the first row. These two rows with their opposite twists, are repeated for the length of the braid.

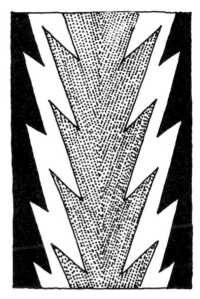

Diagram 20

Detail of a plaited wool band using the Peruvian repp technique from the Nazca culture, Peru, *c.* 400 AD. Denver Art Museum.

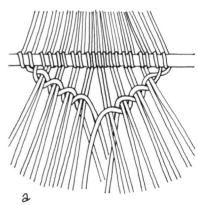

a

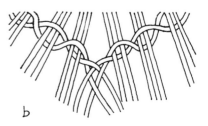

b

Diagram 21

PLAITING WHERE THE ENDS
OF THE THREADS ARE FIXED

Sprang

Sprang is an intricate form of plaiting which is made with threads which are stretched in tension and secured at both ends. Sometimes called twined plaiting, it is a technique in which the lengthways threads are twisted in such a way that a netlike textile is produced. The elasticity of this method of plaiting becomes apparent when the tension of the threads is released and the fabric can be stretched across its width.

There is no weft in sprang. The structure consists entirely of an interlinking of the lengthways or warp threads, worked from either end towards the centre, where a central locking thread holds them in place.

This technique is an ancient one and textile fragments have been excavated which have survived from Ancient Peru, dated around 500 BC, from the Coptic weavers in Egypt dated about the same time, as well as evidence of pieces made in Norway, Denmark and Sweden from the Viking period onwards. Sprang is in fact a Scandinavian word meaning an openwork textile, and it has come to be used as a general descriptive term for this type of plaiting.

Because the textiles produced in this way had great elasticity, they served useful, everyday purposes for clothing, much as knitted fabrics do for us today. The technique was commonly used for different kinds of head-gear, such as caps, hoods, bonnets, hair-nets and snoods, as well as for stockings, mittens, collars and sashes. Due to the nature of fibres being susceptible to disintegration, few pieces of ancient textiles have survived the ravages of time compared with other archeological finds such as pottery, metalwork, jewellery, etc., except where they have been left buried in ideal conditions. The technique of sprang, with a few surviving examples, has been discovered only fairly recently, probably because it was mainly used for everyday articles and, unlike luxury fabrics, the pieces were not treasured but worn out and thrown away. Because it is a rediscovered technique, a number of textiles in museums which were formerly thought to be knitted or lace are now being re-evaluated as sprang. Peter Collingwood's book on *The Techniques of Sprang*, published in 1974, to which I am indebted here, is an in-depth research and practical description of many aspects of sprang which I'm sure has gone a long way to widening knowledge of the subject and showing what creative potential it has.

Preparation

The technique of sprang differs from the various kinds of plaiting described in the first part of this chapter in that the threads are held in tension between two fixed points. There are various ways in which this can be done but the two most common are (i) on a portable frame, (ii) on a backstrap loom. In both cases the tension of the threads needs to be adjustable as the warp threads inevitably tighten and contract as the interlinking between the threads progresses.

Making a frame for sprang

The simple wooden frames described here are suitable for sprang. They must be firm, with strong joints to withstand the tension of the warp. The size can suit your own requirements but, for making braids, a long narrow frame is necessary. A suitable size to begin with would be approximately 1 m × 25 cm (39 in. × 10 in.) inner width and this would be easy to manage as it could be stood on the floor or you could sit with it on your lap, and the top of the frame could be propped against a wall.

Frame with suspended warp rods

This frame has warp rods slung between the top and bottom cross pieces. The two rods are held in position by strong cords tied at the bottom of the frame with adjustable knots, so that the tension of the warp threads can be altered as necessary (Diag. 22). The frame is constructed with the top and bottom cross pieces glued and screwed down on to the side pieces.

Mark each end of the top and bottom frame pieces with a centre cross, through which the screws will be inserted. Drill right through the centre of each cross point. Place wood glue on each end of the side pieces, position the top and bottom pieces over the side pieces and, making sure the frame is at right-angles at each corner, screw down the top and bottom of the frame (Diag. 22a). You will also need two narrow rods, such as wooden dowel, 20 cm long × 6 mm diameter (8 in. × $\frac{1}{4}$ in.), some strong cotton string or cord, and nine thin sticks, fine knitting needles or darning needles.

Cut two lengths of the cord, each about 15 cm (6 in.) longer than double the length of the frame. Attach the centre of each length to the top of the frame with a lark's head knot (Diag. 22b), then make equidistant overhand knots 5 cm (2 in.) down from the inner edges of the top cross piece of the frame, and the same distance up from the inner edge of the bottom cross piece. Making sure each cord is at the same tension, and the overhand knots align with each other, tie a knot with the two ends of each cord around the bottom of the frame.

Insert the two rods above and below the overhand knots, through the cord loops, at the top and bottom of the frame respectively (Diag. 22c).

These cords will support the rods on to which the warp threads are wound and can remain in the frame for a number of different warps.

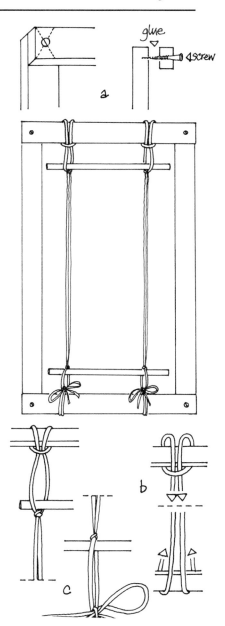

Diagram 22

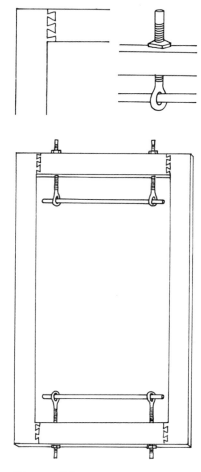

Diagram 23

Frame with tension bolts

An alternative to the frame already described would be to use one which has four tension bolts fixed through the top and bottom cross pieces (Diag. 23). The rods which support the warp are threaded through the eyes of the bolts which can be unscrewed gradually as tension builds up in the warp. When this is done, the rods are let in slightly, so that the warp can slacken.

The frame should be flat and sturdy, with joints which are glued and screwed, or better still, dovetailed for strength. (A suitable size is suggested earlier, on p. 23.) The bolts should be about 15 cm (6 in.) long, with wing nuts. The diameter of the bolts will govern the thickness of wood you need to use for the frame pieces. You will also need two rods 20 cm (8 in.) long, and if you use wooden dowel, take care not to have it too thin; it could bend under the tension between the bolts and the warp. (The cords on the previous frame have an element of elasticity.) Thin metal rods would be very suitable.

Drill holes and screw in the tension bolts at the top and bottom of the frame, allowing space between the inner frame edges and the rods to wind on the warp. The bolts should be extended out from the frame as much as possible at first so that you can unscrew them to let in the rods when necessary.

Warping the frame

You can now begin to wind the warp threads on to the rods of the frame. The instructions here are for a warp of one colour with an even number of threads. (See p. 33 for warping several colours.) For a narrow warp, you could begin with between 12 and 20 threads depending on the thickness of the thread you are using. You can space the warp closely if you want a dense braid, or further apart for a looser, more open structure, but in any case the warp threads can be moved along the rods after warping and the sprang structure will naturally find its own spacing.

Because of the limited space between the rods and the top and bottom pieces of the frame you will obviously only be able to wind around them with a fairly small ball of thread. It is easier if you estimate the number of threads you will need and wind them off length by length from the main spool or ball of thread. Cut the total amount of thread you will need for the warp and wind it into a small ball or around a spool of paper. Start at the bottom left by tying the end of the thread to the lower rod with a temporary knot. Pass the ball of thread up to the top rod, and pass it behind and around it. Now bring it down the frame, and pass it over and around the lower rod. Continue in this way, keeping the tension as even as possible, and the threads evenly spaced and parallel to one another. Finish on the bottom right by temporarily tying the warp to the lower rod (Diag. 24).

With this method of warping it is almost inevitable that some threads will be looser than others. You can now adjust any irregularities by taking hold of a loose thread and pushing the slack along on to the next thread, either up or down depending on whether you are moving to the left or the right. Keep firm hold of each thread in turn, and gradually ease all the slackness out of the far left or far right warp threads. When you are satisfied the warp is even, secure the knots at either end permanently.

Making a backstrap loom for sprang
A backstrap loom is one of the oldest traditional methods of weaving narrow strips of cloth. The warp is stretched between two sticks, one of which is attached to a fixed point and the other to the waist of the weaver. The result of this is that it is the weaver who controls the tension of the warp by sitting or standing upright.

Sprang can be done successfully on a simple loom of this type, although if this is a very new technique to you, you may find that a tensioned warp separate from you on a frame enables you to concentrate more closely on the interlinking of the threads. However, the advantage of a backstrap loom is its absolute simplicity of materials – you just need a few sticks and a belt – and its facility to be rolled up and put away. In the chapter on woven braids on p. 64 I have described how to make and set up a backstrap loom.

Warping a backstrap loom for sprang
The warping process is the same as that already described for a frame on p. 24. To wind the warp for a backstrap loom, you will first need two fixed points around which you can do this. These should be set the correct distance apart for the length of your warp. Two warping posts clamped to a table are ideal, or the top of the clamps themselves would do; failing that two chairs at either end of a table would be satisfactory (see p. 58). Wind the warp in the same sequence as described on p. 24 for winding around the rods of the frame. Having adjusted the tension, slip the two sticks which are the top and bottom rods of the backstrap loom into each end of the warp, and set yourself up with the loom (see p. 65).

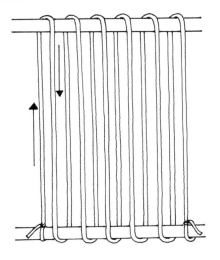

Diagram 24

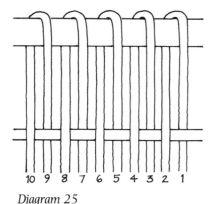

Diagram 25

10 9 8 7 6 5 4 3 2 1

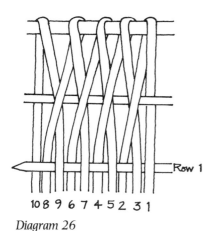

Row 1

10 8 9 6 7 4 5 2 3 1

Diagram 26

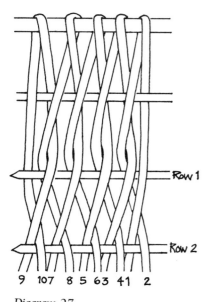

Row 1

Row 2

9   10 7   8 5   6 3   4 1   2

Diagram 27

Final preparation

Now you have your warp set up for sprang, you will also need nine very thin sticks. These are inserted into the most recent rows as the interlacing progresses. The shorter, double-pointed knitting needles are ideal, or long darning needles, but any wooden sticks would do. The finer the threads that you work with, the thinner your sticks will need to be. At this point take one stick and insert it over and under each thread in turn. Start on the right, pass it over the first thread, under the second and so on across the warp (Diag. 25). This stick organizes the threads in their correct order, so, counting from the right, the odd-numbered threads are behind the stick, and are called back threads and the even numbered threads are in front of the stick, and are called front threads.

Single interlinking

There are a number of different methods of interlinking the threads in sprang, so I will concentrate here on describing the basic technique for interlinking the threads in a single twist.

The interlinking takes place in the top half of the warp and is made with a technique which consists of two rows, worked alternately, with the start of each row always on the right. Each row is worked by picking up the back threads in the correct order with the stick held in the right hand, and dropping off the front threads of the left hand. As each interlinking row is made at the top of the warp, a simultaneous row appears at the lower edge. Rows 1 and 2 are worked progressively to the centre of the warp.

Row 1   Put your left hand into the shed in the warp so that the front threads are held in front of your fingers. With a stick in the right hand, pick up the first two back threads (1 and 3) and hold them on the stick. Drop the first front thread (2) from your left hand and slip it behind the stick in your right hand. Pick up the third back thread (5) on the stick and drop the second front thread (4) from your left hand and slip it behind the stick. Pull the threads apart so that you can see them clearly. Continue across the row, picking up each back thread on to the stick and dropping each front thread so that it falls behind the stick. Finish by dropping the last two front threads (Diag. 26).

* Row 1 has two threads in front of the stick at the start of the row and two threads behind it at the end.

Insert a second stick into the shed of the same row and slide the upper one to the top of the warp and the lower one to the botton of the warp. Push the sticks firmly against the threads to hold the interlinked rows made so far.

Row 2 Put your left hand into the shed and with a third stick in your right hand, pick up the first back thread (2) and drop the first front thread (1) so that it lies behind the stick. Pick up the next back thread (4) and drop the next front thread (3). Continue across the warp in this way and finish by dropping the last front thread (Diag. 27).

* Row 2, unlike row 1, has only one thread in front of the stick at the start of the row and one behind at the end.

Insert a fourth stick into the shed of the same row and slide the upper one to the top of the warp and the lower one to the bottom, pushing them against the previous row (see photograph on p. xx). These two rows are repeated alternately, with two sticks left in the warp at either end, after each row. On the fifth row, the first two sticks you inserted can be withdrawn from the warp and re-used in successive rows.

There are two advantages to leaving the sticks in the rows in this way. They enable you to push down and up against the threads after each row, so that an even tension in the sprang is maintained which would otherwise be difficult to regulate.

They can also make it possible to undo rows if a mistake has been made further back. To undo sprang can be tedious, so if you discover a mistake, say three rows back, first of all remove the sticks from the current shed. Then slide the two from the previous row towards the centre of the warp and this will undo that row of interlinking. Remove these two sticks and repeat with the row prior to that, until you have undone the row with the mistake. Take great care, however, to keep the sticks in the row you are now at to the top and bottom of the warp, so that the shed is safely held and you can begin interlinking again.

As you complete one or other of the rows, you may find yourself in doubt about which row to do next. Look down to the lower stick holding the row just completed. If the first two right threads are together and in front of the stick, with the next thread at the back, then you have completed row 1. If only the first right thread is in front of the stick, with the next thread behind, then you have just completed row 2.

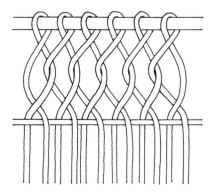

Diagram 28

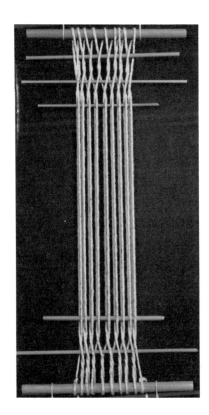

Single interlocking looks like this when rows 1 and 2 have been completed.

Other working methods

As you become more familiar with the technique you will no doubt find a way of manipulating the threads which works well for you. Keep the tension of the warp reasonably taut, but flexible enough for you to be able to pull the threads apart so that you can see them clearly. As the tension builds up after successive rows, release the cord ties at the bottom of the frame (or the tension bolts) so that you can slacken the warp slightly.

An alternative method of working is simply to use the fingers of the right hand instead of a stick to pick up the threads and you may find you have more dexterity working this way. The left hand is still inserted into the shed with the front threads in front of the fingers as already described.

It is also possible to work at the lower end of the warp, especially if your frame is propped in your lap and it is difficult to reach to the top, and certainly when working on a backstrap loom you will need to be working at the beginning of the warp. Keep two sticks in the shed of each row as already described, pushing one down against the threads, and the other up to the top of the warp. Interlink the threads for the next row above the lower stick just inserted. However, if you work at the bottom edge you will need to understand the important difference between the twist of the threads at the lower warp to those at the top, and this is described on p. 29.

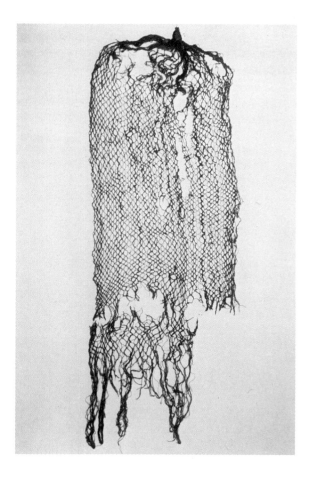

Openwork silk sprang from excavations at Fishamble Street, Dublin. National Museum of Ireland. Height 355 mm, width 125 mm. *c.* 11th century. Photograph J. Pritchard.

S and Z interlinking

As rows 1 and 2 are successively completed, you can begin to see the structure of sprang, and how the threads are twisting. At the top of the warp the threads lie at a slight diagonal to the edges of the braid, sloping from top right to bottom left in each row. This is called a Z twist because of the angle. However, at the bottom of the warp, the threads are twisted in the opposite direction, sloping from top left to bottom right. This is called an S twist (Diag. 29).

In many early examples of sprang, a number of traditional patterns were devised which combined Z and S twists within the rows of interlinking to create complex patterns. I have described how to create some simple patterns which combine S and Z interlinking on p. 30.

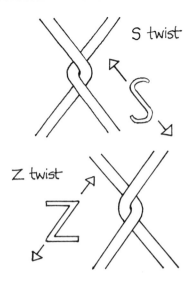

Diagram 29

The final rows

As the rows of interlinking build up and gradually move towards the centre of the warp, it becomes progressively more difficult to pick up the threads. You can work with two sticks or knitting needles near the centre, one to hold the left threads, the other as you have already done, to pick up and keep the threads at the right. Alternatively, you may find it easier to hold a crochet hook, or a latchet hook used for hooked rugs, in your right hand to pick up and hold the right threads after they have been twisted. You may also need to remove the sticks holding the last rows and instead insert a safety cord through the warp to hold the most recently completed row. Push this cord down after each row and pick up the threads above it for the next row.

Single interlinking with an S twist

On p. 27 in rows 1 and 2, I described the basic technique for interlinking threads with a Z twist. Here I will describe how rows of S interlinked threads are made. The essential difference between the two is that with Z twisted threads the back thread is picked up first and the front thread is then dropped, with the right stick, or fingers, doing most of the work. For S-twisted threads the front thread is dropped first and the back thread is then picked up and transferred to the right stick. In S twists, the left fingers make most of the movements. The rows are worked right to left, and if you have already completed several rows of Z interlinking, you will need to have finished with row 2, as described on p. 27.

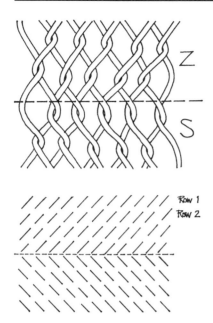

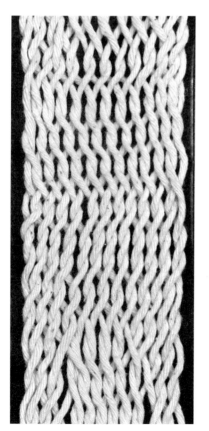

A sprang braid in one colour which combines S and Z interlinking to create subtle patterns.

Row 1   Put your left hand into the warp so that the front threads are held in front of your fingers. Slip your left thumb behind the first two front threads and take hold of the first back thread between your thumb and forefinger. Bring it across to the left, behind the front two threads, and drop them. Pass the back thread in front of the two threads and transfer it on to the right stick. Let the two front threads fall behind the stick. Repeat the movement with the next front thread being dropped, and the next back thread being brought to the left behind it, then in front to be transferred on to the stick. Continue till you reach the last three threads, one in front and two behind the fingers of the left hand. Pick up the two back threads, bring them to the left behind the front thread. Drop the front thread, and transfer the two threads on to the stick.

* Row 1 has two threads at the back at the beginning of the row and two in front at the end of the row. This is the opposite positioning to row 1 for Z interlinking.

Row 2   Put your left hand into the warp. Slip your left thumb behind the first front thread and take hold of the first back thread. Bring it to the left, drop the front thread, and transfer it to the right stick with the same movement as described in row 1 so that you have twisted the back and front threads. Continue in this way with every front and back thread in the warp.

* In row 2, one thread is behind the stick at the beginning and one in front at the end; the opposite to row 2 for Z interlinking.

Making patterns which combine S and Z interlinking
In the method of sprang I have described so far, you can interlink with either a Z or an S twist. In the resulting braid, one half is a mirror of the other half, that is Z interlinking in the top half automatically produces S interlinking in the bottom half, or vice versa. It is also possible to combine the two kinds of interlinking within the rows to create patterns. In a braid using threads of one colour these will appear as subtle patterning on the surface (see photograph on p. 30). Patterns can appear more dramatic if different coloured threads are used (see photograph facing p. 32).

First of all, try making horizontal stripes of complete rows of S and Z interlinking. You will need to make the number of rows in multiples of two as each method needs two completed rows. Diag. 30 shows how you can design these patterns on paper and make four rows of Z interlinking followed by four rows of S interlinking.

Patterns of S interlinking can be made within rows of Z interlinking as shown in Diag. 31. To make a diamond pattern, the interlinking is worked in the following way. After you have interlinked several threads in a Z twist, the front thread is over the right stick followed by a back thread behind it. To change to S twist, first drop the next front thread from the left hand. Slide the thumb and forefinger of your left hand behind the next back thread which follows the front thread you have just dropped. Take hold of the dropped front thread between your thumb and forefinger, pull it to the left behind the back thread, then pass it in front of the back thread and transfer it on to the right stick. Let the back thread fall behind the right stick. If you find it difficult keeping the thread on the right stick, use the fingers of your right hand to work with instead. Complete the row with Z-interlinked threads. In the second row of the diamond pattern, you will interlink one less thread in a Z twist to the right and left of the pattern, as the S twisted threads will increase to three on this row. You can recognize the point where you stop Z interlinking by looking for two threads lying together behind the left fingers in this row. Include one of these as a Z twist. Then you are ready to change to S twists. Make three S-twisted threads, then finish the row with Z-interlinked threads. Continue in this way, following the pattern chart row by row (Diag. 31) to make a diamond, remembering that the Z-interlinked threads you begin and end with and the S interlinking in the centre are still worked as rows 1 and 2 alternately.

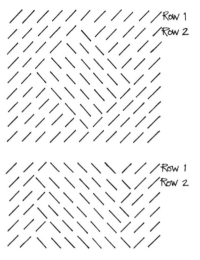

Diagram 31

Securing the threads at the meeting point
When you are about 4 cm (1½ in.) from the middle of the warp, the threads need to be secured. If you were to remove the sticks immediately after the final row, the threads would untwist completely, so some method of holding the twisted threads must be made. I will describe three ways to do this here.

Woven threads
The simplest method is to weave one thread through the warp to secure the interlinking. Alternatively, three threads can be woven in, each one weaving over and under warp threads in opposite rows, with the ends tied in overhand knots (Diag. 32). This method allows for a degree of widthways stretch in the sprang. If you want the warp threads held closely together, weave three rows with a single thread, and darn the ends along the selvedge. Remove the stick when the threads are secured.

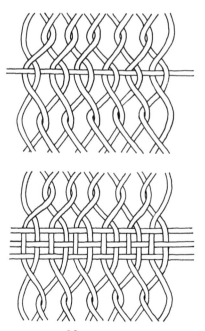

Diagram 32

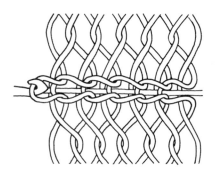

Diagram 33

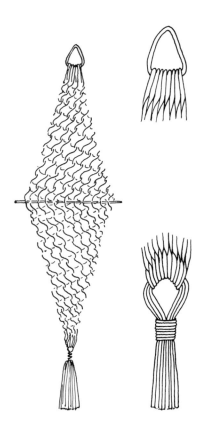

Diagram 34

Chaining

You will need a crochet hook to do this. The advantage of this method is that it has the most elasticity, so if you want your sprang braid to stretch widthways, this is very suitable. Work on the threads in front of the stick in the shed of the final row, starting on the right. Slide the hook behind threads 1 and 2 from right to left. Catch thread 2 in the hook and pull it out at the right, under thread 1. Now slide it under thread 3 and pull it back under thread 2. Continue across the row, leave the hook in the last loop (Diag. 33). Turn the frame round and work across the threads in front of the stick on this side of the braid. Tie the last loop to the selvedge.

A rod

You can insert a metal, wooden or perspex rod into the final row at the centre of the warp, particularly if you want to hang your sprang braid as a decorative piece. Stretch the centre threads on the rod slightly to show the interlinked structure (Diag. 34).

Finishing off the sprang braid

Using the same type of thread as the warp, attach a length at either end by threading it through the loops on the top and bottom rods. Slide the warp off the rods and tie the ends. The ends of the braid can be made decorative by adding several threads and wrapping them to make tassels (Diag. 34) and see p. 74. As the tension of the warp is released, the sprang braid will twist, so it is necessary to press it. Place the braid on an ironing board, pin it down, and gently steam-press until it is flat.

Colour plate: Plaited braids, l to r: (1) lightning finger braid, (2) Hopi wedding sash, (3) sprang braid in 2 colours, (4) chevron finger braid, (5) diagonal striped finger braids, and (6) twined braid.

Making a warp with different coloured threads

A warp for sprang can also be wound in a variety of colours. Multi-coloured sashes and belts were made in sprang in Ancient Egyptian times by the Copts, and pieces are still made in this way today in Pakistan.

The threads are wound in a continuous warp as described on p. 24 and the colour changes are made by knotting the different threads to one another at the upper or lower rods (see p. 36). You can also wind coloured threads around the rods in such a way as to avoid having a number of knots, and I will describe two methods here.

Diag. 35 shows how to wind a striped warp based on four threads in colour A and four in colour B. The starting and finishing ends are secured to the lower rod, but during the winding of the warp, each colour is carried along the lower rod and continued when needed. Alternate warp threads of A and B can be wound in a similar way, starting with the two ends tied alongside one another at the start; you then wind them round the rods together until they are finally secured at the right of the lower rod (Diag. 35).

It is also possible to rearrange the colours by temporarily inserting two sticks at the top of the warp, over and under the threads. If you do this with an AB/AB warp you can get variations of AA/BB or AAA/BBB (Diag. 36). The sticks hold the threads in the correct order for the first interlinking row. In this case it is easier to begin with a row-2 Z-interlinking row, where you pick up the first back thread and drop the next front thread, and so on (see p. 27). Follow this with row 1 and, when you have completed this row, remove the two sticks temporarily inserted at the top of the warp and push the sticks holding the two interlinking rows up to the top rod. Any cross-over of the warp threads resulting from their being rearranged will be pushed to the very top and bottom of the warp and can be sorted out when the rods are eventually removed. Continue as usual with alternate interlinking rows.

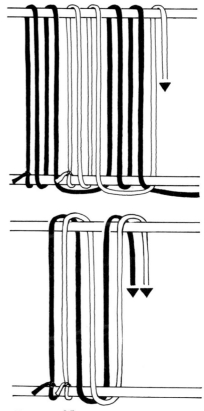

Diagram 35

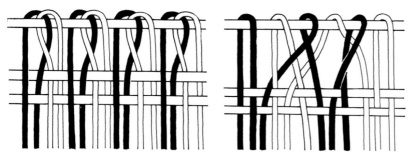

Diagram 36

Colour plate: Knotted braids, l to r: (1 & 2) with diagonal clove hitches, (3) with horizontal clove hitches, (4) with horizontal and vertical clove hitches, and (5) with diagonal clove hitches and alternating chains.

The Hopi wedding sash in two colours.

Hopi wedding sash

The Hopi Indians of N. America have for centuries used a technique of interlacing threads to make a wedding sash, and the manner in which it is worked is similar to sprang. Traditionally made in a natural handspun cotton, it is woven by the men in the bridegroom's family as a gift for the bride. The sash is usually about 23 cm wide by nearly 3 m long (9 in. × 9 ft.), including long fringes at either end. The Hopi method of plaiting the sash is to attach the top rod holding the warp to the wall of the house with the other rod secured by a heavy stone on the floor, so that the warp is stretched horizontally above the floor. The person plaiting the sash sits alongside the warp. The warp for a Hopi sash can just as well be set up on a frame of the same type as that described on p. 23 for sprang.

There are some fundamental differences between the Hopi sash and sprang. Firstly, the threads in sprang interlink around one another in a twisted zig-zag path which runs down the length of the warp. However, in the Hopi sash, the threads cross one another in a diagonal path from one edge of the warp to the other and back again. Rather than making a twist around one another, the threads pass over and under each other in a particular sequence. To differentiate between the two, I will describe the Hopi method as interlacing, as it bears a closer relation to weaving, and to the plaiting techniques described in the first part of this chapter. Secondly, the threads are interlaced on the front warp only, i.e. the threads stretched in front of the two rods. This means the front threads and back threads are considered separately, unlike sprang (Diag. 39). The interlacing starts at the meeting point on the front warp and extends either side of it to the ends of the sash, where the threads are cut (Diag. 39). There are also methods of sprang made in this way, often called circular warp sprang. Thirdly, the two rows repeated throughout the Hopi sash differ not only in their picking-up sequence but also in the way that they are worked first right to left, then left to right.

Warping the frame

Either of the frames described on pp. 23 and 24 are suitable for plaiting a Hopi sash. The warp is wound around the upper and lower rods, but in this case attach the first end with a temporary knot to the top left of the upper rod and wind down, behind and over the lower rod, then up and over the upper rod and so on (Diag. 37). The number of threads for the Hopi sash needs to be an even number of threads which are divisible by three with an additional thread, counting across on the front threads. For example, a narrow braid could consist of 6 groups of three threads, 18, plus one, so you would wind your warp to have 19 threads on the front and 19 on the back. Maintain an even tension as you wind the warp around the rods and then secure the two ends as follows. Because this is a circular warp, you will be interlacing the threads around the warp so that, as the rows build up you will push them from the front to the back; that is the whole warp will be moved around the rods. This means that the ends cannot be attached to the rods. A temporary join is therefore made with the ends, and later when the sash is completed, the ends can be neatly knotted and darned in. To make the temporary join, half-hitch each end to its neighbour thread and knot them together (Diag. 38). This will be the centre meeting point of the sash.

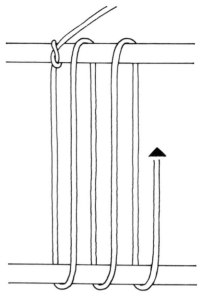

Diagram 37

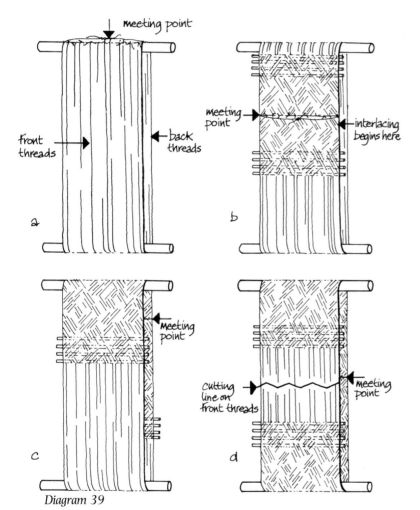

Diagram 39

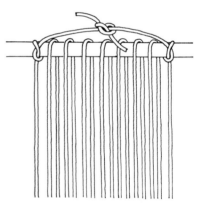

Diagram 38

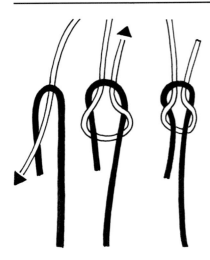

Diagram 40

Winding a warp of two colours

Striking patterns can be made in the Hopi sash by using two or more colours. The braid in photograph facing p. 32 was made in navy and yellow, using a total of 25 warp threads, counting across the front warp. The colours were arranged in the following order: 3N/3Y/3N/3Y/3Y/3N/3Y/4N.

The warp threads are wound around the rods in the way already described, except that the different colours are knotted to one another with a weaver's knot (Diag. 40) as the warp passes over the upper rod. Join the first and last warp thread as shown in Diag. 38. The ends of the knots can be trimmed or darned into the sash when it is completed.

Interlacing the threads

You will need eight thin sticks, as described for sprang, which will hold the most recently completed rows on the front warp, and with which you can push the interlaced threads row by row round to the back. The length of these sticks will, however, need to be shorter than the rods in the frame, so you can slide them over and around the rods.

Before you start interlacing the threads, gently slide the meeting point of the warp down a little so that it is within easy reach (Diag. 39b). Remember you are working on the front threads only.

Row 1   Starting on the right, pass the first thread behind the next three and slip it on to a stick. Pick up the next two threads and slip them on to a stick as well so that you now have three threads behind the stick and three in front. Continue in this way with all the threads until at the end of the row you have one thread behind the stick (Diag. 41). Insert another stick into the same shed, below the first one. Leave the upper one in place, and slide the lower one down the warp, carefully over and around the bottom rod, up the back warp, over and around the top rod and close to the meeting point. Push both sticks firmly against either side of the meeting point.

Row 2   Start on the left with a third stick. Pass the first thread, which has the last thread behind the stick in row 1, behind the next three threads and pick it up on to the stick. Pick up the next two threads so that you have three behind and three in front. Continue in this way, finishing with one thread behind the stick (Diag. 41). Insert a fourth stick below it, in the same shed, and push the lower stick around the warp, as you did in row 1, so that you now have four sticks holding the two rows either side of the meeting point.

Rows 1 and 2 are repeated continuously. When you have four sticks inserted either side of the meeting point, you can begin to withdraw the first ones and re-use them in successive rows. Adjust the tension of the cords holding the rods or the tension bolts, depending on which kind of frame you are working on, as the warp threads will tighten up. As the interlacing rows build up, gradually slide the warp up and over the top rod so that the meeting point moves to the back, and the area of warp you are working on is still within easy reach (Diag. 39c).

Finishing off

In the last stages of making the sash, the interlacing will extend over both rods, leaving an area of unworked threads in the middle of the front warp (Diag. 39d). Decide on the length of fringes you want and cut through the warp as shown in Diag. 39d. The sticks are removed and the ends can be plaited, knotted or wrapped to complete the sash (see p. 71). The meeting point is now the centre of the sash. The original knotted ends can now be either trimmed, or undone and secured by darning them alongside the interlaced threads.

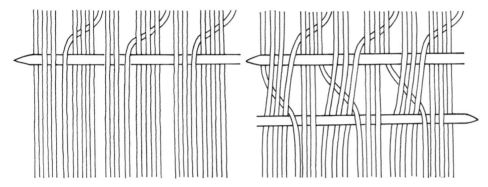

Diagram 41

Knotted braids

Tying knots is a skill which has been a useful part of everyday life since the earliest civilizations began, and one which most of us use when we need to without a great deal of thought. When peoples from ancient cultures discovered the possibilities of natural, pliable fibres and raw materials, how they could build their huts, their rafts and canoes, make clothing and devise traps for food, then the realization that knots could be tied in the fibres to hold and secure the work must have come soon after. Now when we tie a shoelace, a ribbon or a scarf, we probably pay little attention to how or from where that knot originated.

Knotting consists of one or more elements, in which loops are made and pulled through to hold the structure firm. It may originally have been a purely functional craft, but in certain early cultures, particularly in Ancient Peru where textiles were highly developed, its decorative qualities were also realized. In recent history it is with the sea and sailors that knotting has been most closely associated, and by the nineteenth century fancy knotting was a widespread and competitive interest amongst merchant seamen with many long hours at sea to fill. In the Victorian era the interest in fancy knots grew with a desire to ornament and decorate furnishings and interiors, and it was at this time that macramé, from an Arabic word for fringe or veil, came to be the overall description for all kinds of knotted work.

In this chapter I have concentrated on how you can use a variety of knots to make braids, starting with simple cords which use only a single thread and are made on your fingers, to all sorts of intricate fancy braids, flat, round, and with decorative edges, using a number of threads worked on a board. The type of thread you use can vary from very fine cotton, even wire, to heavy cord or rope, but in the main avoid very slippery materials which will not hold the knots. Matt cotton twine is ideal for first projects and samples. The tension of your knots will be personal to you; a braid can be open and loose, or tight and firm, depending on the materials, its purpose and how you want the final appearance to be.

Braid knotted in diagonal clove hitches, see p. 46.

Finger knotting with a single thread

A variety of knotted cords and braids can be made by the simple method of finger manipulating a single continuous thread, and I have described three ways to do this in the first section. Obviously the flexibility of your fingers is important with this kind of knotting as you are not only making loops and pulling the thread through to form the knots, but also having to adjust the tension as you work, and all on your hand! Use a pliable, reasonably thick thread to start with, such as soft cotton twine, until you have mastered the techniques. The great advantage of finger knotting is that you can pick it up and do it anywhere, whether sitting in the park or waiting for an appointment, and then put it back in your pocket again! It can be most relaxing and therapeutic.

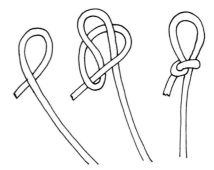

Diagram 42

Finger or monkey chain

This is probably one of the original and most universal methods of making a chain braid with a single element. As it uses a single strand, you can work straight off the spool or ball of whichever type of thread you have chosen.

Although I have described it here as a finger chain, as it most probably was originally devised, you will probably recognize it as a crochet chain which can be made with a hook.

Start with a slip knot (Diag. 42). Put your fingers through the loop of the slip knot and pull up another loop from the continuous length of thread. Use your fingers like a hook to pull the second loop through the original one. Tighten. Continue making further loops in this way (Diag. 43). To finish, cut the thread, and pull through the last loop and tighten (photograph on p. 40)

This chain is ideal for temporarily shortening longer threads, as it can easily be pulled out again; for example, on window blind cords or, if you weave, to shorten long warp threads whilst preparing and threading the loom.

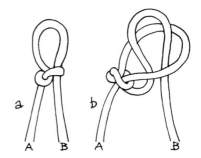

Diagram 43

Triangular cord

Take a length of thread and tie a slip knot in the centre (Diag. 44a). Make the two ends of equal length from the knot, and label them A and B. Take thread A and pass it behind B. Form a loop with it and pass it through the original loop of the slip knot (Diag. 44b). Tighten the original loop by pulling thread B. Adjust the second loop by pulling thread A. Now make a loop with thread B. Slip it through the loop just made and tighten by first pulling A, then adjusting the new loop by pulling B. Keep making loops alternately with A and B through one another in this way, till you have a cord the length you want. To finish, simply pass one end of thread through the other loop and tighten (photograph on page 40).

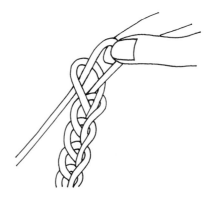

Diagram 44

Three finger knotted braids . Left to right:
(1) Finger or monkey chain
(2) Triangular cord
(3) Square cord.

Square cord

This cord is worked on a single thread wrapped around the fingers of your hand, and can be worked directly from a ball of yarn or cotton. The beginning of the thread is held between the thumb and the palm of your hand, and the knots are worked along the rest of the thread. Start by winding the thread up from the end held in the palm of your hand between fingers 1 and 2, around finger 1 and behind finger 2.

Now take the thread over finger 2 and back behind finger 1, so that it is at the front of your hand again. Lift the lower loop on finger 1 over the upper loop. Pull the beginning of the thread to tighten the knot. The second step is to pass the thread back between fingers 1 and 2 and around the front of finger 2. Lift the lower loop on finger 2 over the upper loop and pull to tighten. These two steps are repeated continuously to make a square cord (Diag. 45). Look carefully to see the path the thread is taking so that you can see where to tighten. You may find it easier to pull on the opposite loop to the one you have just made, before pulling on the thread itself. If you find it difficult working this braid on your fingers, try placing the thread on a two-pronged twig.

To finish off, cut the thread with an allowance of 10 cm (4 in.), slip both loops off your fingers, pass the end through the left loop then back across through the right loop and pull tight (photograph on this page).

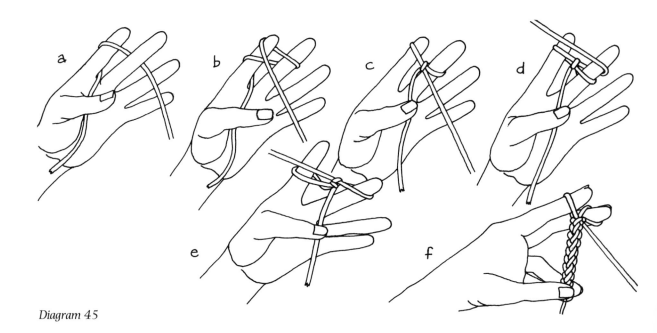

Diagram 45

Knotting with several separate threads

Tying knots with several separate threads, or macramé as it is usually described, offers a tremendous range of possibilities for braidmaking. A knotted braid in traditional nautical terms is described as a sinnet or sennet, and many of the macramé knots described here owe their origins to the skill and ingenuity of sailors and fishermen.

Length of threads
You can try a short sample length first, using cotton twine or string, and from this estimate the length of thread to be cut for the finished item you want to make. Macramé braids take fairly long lengths for the knot-tying threads; approximately seven to eight times the finished length required. These lengths, when mounted on to a supporting thread with lark's head knots or started from a centre loop, will give you two working threads from each length.

Working on a board
Knotted braids need organization of the threads and care with the tension of the knots, so you will almost certainly find knotting is made easier if you use a piece of softboard or a hard cushion as your work surface (see photograph below). The size should be about 30 cm (12 in.) square and the surface can be covered with plain fabric so that you can see your work easily. The threads can be held in place with pins: macramé T-pins which are extra long, or glass-headed steel pins.

Knotted braids can be made more easily if you work on a piece of softboard, keeping the threads in position with pins.

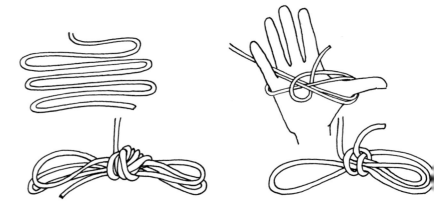

Diagram 46

Mounting threads

When you are working with a number of separate threads, you can mount each length on to a supporting thread with a lark's head knot. For just two or four threads, you can simply pin them in position through the loop at the centre of each length of thread, and start knotting from there. If you are making a braided edging to a fabric or for furnishings, loop the threads through with a hook or needle (Diag. 46).

Tying up long threads

If you are making long braids, the threads are very long when you first begin to knot them. You will need to bundle them up to avoid getting them tangled, and to make them easier to work with. One method is to tie the individual threads in butterflies. Allow about 30–46 cm (12–18 in.) from the start of each thread, and wind up the rest in a figure of eight around your thumb and forefinger (Diag. 46). You can secure the butterfly of thread either by half-hitching the end around the centre of the butterfly twice or by securing it with an elastic band. The thread can easily be pulled out as you need more, during the knotting.

For thicker, heavier threads, wind up the thread from the cut end in concertina fashion, then secure with a loose overhand knot (Diag. 47). You will need to undo the knot each time you want to lengthen the thread.

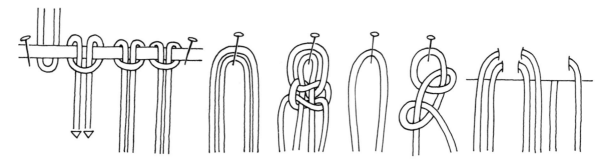

Diagram 47

Finishing braids

With the finger-knotted braids made from a single thread, the end that you finish with can be used to attach the braid to a blind or a light-pull for example. Finer braids could be appliquéd to fabric as a decorative edging or used as loop fastenings on a dress or jacket. Making your own braids can enable you to co-ordinate the colours and threads you work with to a specific project you have planned.

The half-hitch

The half-hitch is the most basic knot, and there are a number of variations combining single, double or groups of threads which can be used for making braids. Experiment with this knot to discover what the possibilities are and, as braids using the half-hitch are quick to produce, it is ideal for light-pulls, window-blind cords and decorative edgings for furnishings.

The spiral hitch or corkscrew bar is made by repeatedly tying the right thread around the left, keeping the latter taut as you knot. The hitches should be pulled tightly and will gradually twist around the left thread to make an attractive spiral braid.

The buttonhole bar is made in the same way as the spiral hitch but the hitches should be slightly looser and held firmly to the right to prevent twisting (Diag. 48a). This braid needs to be stitched flat on to fabric or furnishings to keep its shape.

The alternating chain or seesaw knot is made with two single threads, and consists of single half-hitches tied alternately by one thread around the other (Diag. 49a). The alternating chain can also be made with two double threads or any even number in two groups to make a thicker, chunkier cord. If the outer single tying threads are alternately looped around two centre holding cords, a flatter braid will be made (Diag. 49b).

The shell-bar is a very decorative braid tied with four threads, using two as tying threads and two as centre holding cords. Start by tying five hitches around the centre holding threads with the left thread. Keep the centre threads taut as you work. Then tie five hitches with the right thread around the centre cords. Pin the braid to your board as you work to prevent it from twisting (Diag. 48b).

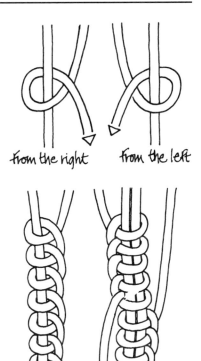

from the right   *from the left*

a   *b*

Diagram 48

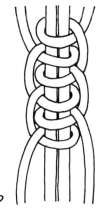

Diagram 49   *a*   *b*

Left to right: (*1*) the spiral hitch or corkscrew bar (*2*) the alternating chain (*3*) the shell bar.

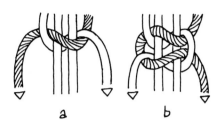

a   b

Diagram 50

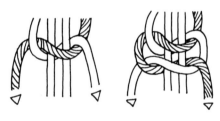

Diagram 51

Square knot

The square knot is one of the main knots in macramé. It is made with four separate threads; the outer two are the tying threads, whilst the centre two are passive holding cords. To make a sennit of square knots, work on a board with pins, as described on p. 41 and keep the holding cords taut by pinning or clipping them to the board, so that you can concentrate on tying with the outer threads. The four threads are first mounted on to a holding cord with a lark's head knot (see mounting threads, p. 42). Wind the threads into bundles as described on p. 42 so that you can work more easily.

The square knot consists of two main steps. First, take the right hand thread **over** the centre two and behind the left thread. Pick up the left thread and pass it diagonally **under** the centre two threads, and out through the right-hand space, over the right thread (Diag. 50a). Tighten the threads to complete the first step. Now take the right hand cord and pass it **under** the centre two threads and over the left thread. Pick up the left thread and pass it diagonally **over** the centre threads and down through the right hand space behind the right thread (Diag. 50b). Tighten the threads to complete the square knot. Repeat these steps for a flat braid (photograph on p. 45).

Half-knot

The half-knot consists of only one of the steps used for the square knot, tied repeatedly (Diag. 51). Follow the instructions for the first step of the square knot described above, and repeat five times. At this stage the braid will automatically begin to twist, so change the positions of the right and left threads, and then continue tying another five half-knots. Repeat in this way to make a spiral braid (photograph on p. 45).

Variations of the square knot

There are many variations of the basic square knot for braidmaking. The knots can be spaced out or pushed closely together, several threads can be knotted around the centre holding threads in a sequence or there can be more threads kept at the centre. The tying and holding threads can switch positions and all kinds of effects can be created with the use of differently coloured threads.

In the spaced square knot, you can control the distance between the knots to get a different effect. In the photograph on p. 45 the knots are tied at regular intervals to make an open sennit. Or slide the knots up the centre threads after tying them to make a sennit with a picot edge (see photograph on p. 45). A different sennit can be made by switching the position of the centre and outer threads after each square knot has been tied.

A more intricate lacy square-knot sennit using eight threads is illustrated in the photograph on p. 45. Number the threads 1–8 from left to right. Begin by tying a square knot with the centre four threads, 3, 4, 5 and 6. Keep the threads flat on the board in the correct order and now pick up threads 2 and 7, and taking them above 3 and 6, tie another square knot around the centre two threads, 4 and 5. Still with 4 and 5 as the centre holding threads, tie a square knot using the outermost threads 1 and 8.

You can now see that the loops which frame the centre square knots are brought to the centre consecutively to give a lacy edge to the braid. To make the most effect with this, keep the loops fairly loose each time you tie a square knot. To continue the pattern, tie another square knot with 1, 4, 5 and 8. Keep the threads flat as they now are and pick up 2 and 7, take them above 1 and 8 and tie a square knot with 2, 4, 5 and 7. Finally tie a knot with 3, 4, 5 and 6. These six knots make the complete pattern. To make a sennit, repeat the six knots of the pattern (photograph below).

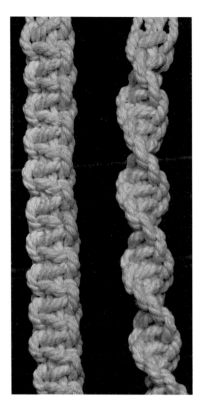

Three sennits showing variations of the basic square knot.
Left to right: (*1*) spaced square knot (*2*) Sennit with picot edge
(*3*) Lacy square knot sennit.

Left to right: (*1*) the square knot
(*2*) the half knot.

The clove hitch

The clove hitch, sometimes called the double half-hitch, is made by tying two loops with one thread around another which acts as the knot bearer or holding cord. The basic knot or hitch is described on p. 43 but here in the clove hitch it is tied twice. The holding cord decides the direction of the knots and can be placed horizontally or diagonally. A third variation is the vertical clove hitch in which one thread acts as a knotting thread throughout and is hitched in turn around the vertical holding cords.

When making clove hitches it is most important to keep the holding cord taut and in the direction you are tying. Pin it to the board in the exact position you want to start, and use pins to hold the knots in position as you work.

Horizontal clove hitch

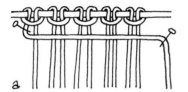

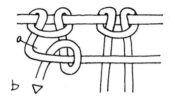

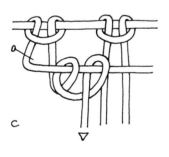

To begin tying a row of horizontal clove hitches from left to right, the far left thread is placed **over** the other threads horizontally, with pins to hold it in position (Diag. 52a). The next left thread is then looped around it twice (Diag. 52b and c). Each hitch should be pulled tight and firm before moving onto the next thread. When a row is complete, the holding cord can be turned and brought back for a right-to-left row in which the hitches are tied right to left (Diag. 53d and e). These can be repeated for a pattern of several rows of hitches. The repeating pattern of rows does mean, however, that you are using the same thread repeatedly as the holding cord, so it will be used up more quickly than the other threads. Take this into account when mounting the threads for a braid, by allowing 12–14 times the finished length, rather than 8. Continuous rows of horizontal hitches can also be worked repeatedly from the left or the right edge, but bear in mind that this will give slanting edges to the rows of knots (Diag. 53f). You can make this a feature of a braid by working several rows in one direction, then in the other, to make a zig-zag design.

Diagonal clove hitch

This is knotted in the same way as the horizontal hitch but the holding cord is placed diagonally across the tying threads (Diag. 54g and h). The diagonal holding cords can be positioned in different sequences to give a wide variety of patterns and, if the holding cords are crossed over, or arranged symmetrically either side of the centre of groups of threads, you can make cross and diamond patterns. Some ideas are shown in the samplers in the photograph facing p. 33.

Diagram 52

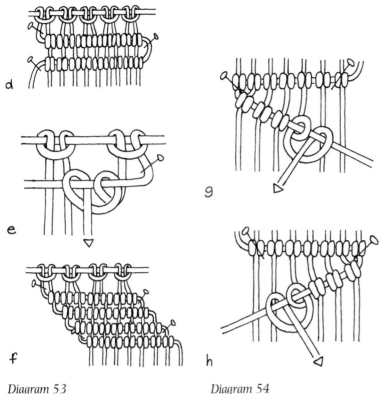

d

e

f

Diagram 53

g

h

Diagram 54

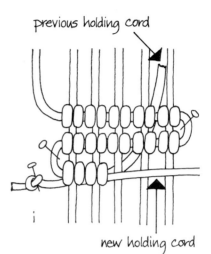

previous holding cord

i

new holding cord

Running out of threads

It is possible to add in new threads when tying horizontal and diagonal hitches. To add a new holding cord, tuck the end you have run short of to the back. Tie an overhand knot in a new thread, and pin it to the board at the side of your work. Bring in the new thread alongside your previous holding cord and begin to hitch around it from where you had left off and continue (Diag. 55i). It is best to make the join in the middle of a row rather than at the edges, so that it won't show.

If a tying thread runs out, then tuck the short end to the back. Tie an overhand knot in a new thread and pin it to the board above and behind the row of knots you are working on. Bring the new thread down and then to the front at the point where you want to recommence knotting and again, making any join in the middle of a row (Diag. 55j). In both cases the ends can be trimmed and darned into the back of the knots. You can also dab the ends with fabric glue for additional strength.

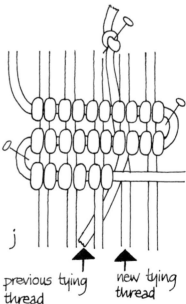

j

previous tying thread

new tying thread

Diagram 55

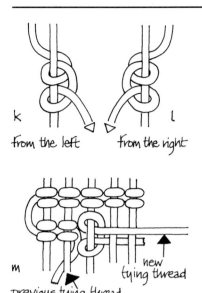

k   from the left   from the right   l

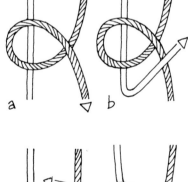

m   previous tying thread   new tying thread

Diagram 56

The vertical clove hitch

In the vertical clove hitch the roles of the threads described in the horizontal and the diagonal hitches are reversed and one thread does all the tying whilst the other vertical threads act as holding cords in turn. Consequently the direction of the hitch is different and a series of rows produces a surface with a vertical rib.

To tie vertical hitches from left to right, begin with the far left thread as a tying thread and tie two hitches around the next thread which is now the holding cord (Diag. 56k). Pull the knot tight and move the tying thread under the next (third) thread and make another vertical hitch. You can also start on the right and make hitches across to the left (Diag. 56l).

New threads can be added in, if you run short, as already described above. With the vertical hitch though, a new holding cord would have to be pinned above and behind the knots and brought down vertically, whereas tying threads can be attached to the holding cord with a lark's head knot. If you are tying knots with single threads, make your lark's head knot with a short end which can be darned in, and a long end which will be your new thread (Diag. 56m). For double threads, tie on your new thread doubled with the lark's head knot in the centre in the usual way, to give you two new threads.

Colour and pattern with clove hitches

Clove hitches make very dense and firm knots and can be used to produce a wide variety of patterns and motifs. This can be made even more attractive by using differently coloured threads to emphasize the patterns the knots make. See the braids in the photograph facing p. 33 which show some of the possibilities there are for designing and making braids with clove hitch knots.

Josephine knot

The Josephine knot is a graceful flat knot which can be repeated in various patterns. It is made with two threads or two groups of threads, and with the latter all the threads should be kept flat and parallel in the completed knot.

Diag. 57 a–d shows the four steps involved in making a Josephine knot. Braids using repeating knots can be made but alternate the tying direction each time; that is, start looping with the right thread for the first knot, then the left thread for the next, otherwise the braid will twist.

a   b

c   d

Diagram 57

Colour plate: Looped braids, l to r: (1) twisted crochet cord, (2) crocheted braid with triangular motif, (3) tubular knitted braid, (4) scalloped crocheted braid, and (5) tubular knitted braids plaited together.

Colour plate overleaf: Tablet woven braids, top to bottom: (1) braid using Method 1 design with 4 turns each way, (2) double-faced lettered braid, (3) double-faced patterned braid, (4 & 6) using Method 1 design with turns in l direction only, and (5) braid using chart on p. 61 with different turning sequences.

Chinese priest and lantern cords

The Chinese perfected flat knots such as the Josephine knot and others related to it in the cords worn by Buddhist priests, as part of their religious costume. They may also have been used as temple ornaments, particularly in Tibet, but the origins of these beautiful cords are uncertain. According to the *Ashley Book of Knots*, by Clifford Ashley, the cords were generally made in a heavy silk-covered cord, about 1.50 m (5 ft.) long. The variety of knots, usually numbering eight or nine, were made from two pairs or groups of cords which always ran parallel along the cord between each knot and culminated in heavy tassels.

If you study these knots and try some samples, you will find that the path each thread takes around the other is always over and under alternately when the complete knot has been tied. If you are going to repeat the knots in a braid, remember to alternate the tying directions for each successive knot, as described for the Josephine knot, to prevent the braid from twisting.

As well as the priest cords, the Chinese also made beautiful cords to hang lanterns by in the temples. These cords combined the use of silk, cotton, gold and silver threads and incorporated semi-precious stones as well as glass and metal ornaments in and between the knots. One of the simplest and most often used was the Chinese crown knot (Diag. 57).

Illustrated here (Diags. 58 and 59) are some of the knots used in Chinese cords, and the intertwining of the threads, especially when made in strong, silky cord and weighted with tassels, would make attractive blind or light-pulls and decorative hanging braids for curtains and tie-backs.

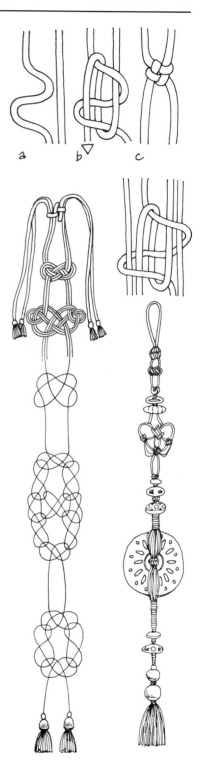

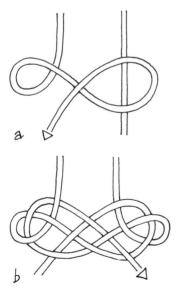

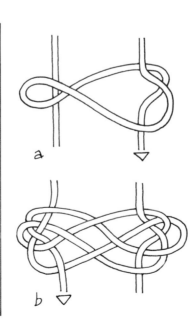

Diagram 58

Diagram 59

Looped braids

If we look at the development of textiles and how they are constructed, the techniques used seem to fall into two main categories: those which are produced with one thread such as netting, and those which use two or more sets of threads as in plaiting, macramé and weaving.

The one-thread system employs a repeated movement in which loops are made and this can be done in two ways. The thread can be a limited length, so the loops are made by drawing the end through the previous loop. This is how the earliest kinds of network originated, and some forms of lace developed this further. The loops can be interlinked to form a mesh or secured with knots in the thread. The other form of single-thread construction is worked with a continuous thread by pulling that part of the thread nearest to the last loop through it to make the next one. This is most familiar to us as both knitting and crochet and, although neither of these methods may be immediately apparent as a means of making braids, I will describe in this chapter a few looping techniques which are very successful as cords and braids.

Tubular knitting

There are references to knitting having been established as a craft in ancient times, for example, in Egypt and Ancient Peru, although it is by no means certain how the pieces were made. Very early pieces had the appearance of knitting but may well have been network or sprang (see p. 22) and the use of needles, as we know it today, may not have been employed then. It would seem that the nomads of Arabia produced one of the earliest forms of knitting frame, in the form of a wooden spool with bone pegs, on which knitting in the round could be made to produce socks and stockings. This method of knitting can, in its simplest form, be used to make tubular braids, the number and spacing of the pegs deciding the size and complexity of the looping.

The simplest spool for this kind of knitting can be a wooden cotton reel, with four nails set around the hole at the top (Diag. 60). Attach one end of your thread, which can be wool, cotton, silk or linen with a slip knot to one nail and pass the end down through the centre hole of the reel. Make loops around the other three nails in turn. The knitting is started by passing the continuous thread around the first nail, and with a needle or fine crochet hook, lifting the lower loop over the thread and the nail and dropping it towards the centre. This is one knitted stitch. Continue passing the thread

Tubular knitted braids, left, in linen thread, and right, in space-dyed yarn.

around each nail in turn and making a stitch each time, gradually pulling on the end at the bottom of the reel until the tube of knitting emerges and grows in length.

When the braid is the length you want, cut the thread leaving an end 10 cm (4 in.) long. Carefully lift the loops off the nails and pull the braid through the reel. Use a needle to thread the end through each of the loops, pull them tightly together and darn the end into the braid.

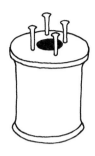

The thickness of the knitted braid depends on the type of thread you work with as well as the size, spacing and number of nails on the spool. You can fix more nails to the spool or the spool itself can be larger, for example, a bamboo or cardboard tube could be used with a wooden top fitted tightly into one end with nails attached. On this scale, your yarn would need to be considerably thicker.

A much firmer braid can be made by inserting a cord down the centre hole which acts as a core around which the knitting is made. Very interesting braids can be knitted using different textured threads, by changing colours in the continuous thread (knot one end to a new with a weaver's knot (see p. 36)) or by using space-dyed yarn (see photograph facing p. 48). Separate knitted tubes can be plaited together, using some of the plaiting techniques described in the first chapter (see photograph facing p.48).

Crochet braids

Crochet is made with a continuous thread and a hook, its name being derived from the French word 'crochét' which means a hook. The early history is difficult to trace but it seems that it may have developed from netting and lacemaking with the idea that these crafts could be further embellished with surface decoration of loops, knots and motifs made with a hooked needle. However it began, crochet had become firmly established as a craft in its own right by the sixteenth century, mainly carried out by nuns. They taught their skills to pupils, until crochet works, particularly lace, became highly desired by the wives and daughters of the wealthy, and being able to crochet was considered an accomplishment no well-to-do lady should be without.

In the reign of Queen Victoria all sorts of crochet work, from antimacassars to fringed lampshades, were in vogue, but it subsequently lost popularity for a while and, like macramé, didn't inspire much interest until the 1950s onwards.

I have included two cords and two braids made in crochet here, to indicate the possibilities there are in crochet for braidmaking. Your choice of hook should equate in size with the thread you use. A large hook with fine thread will make flimsy braids, and a small hook with thick thread will make braids which are dense and stiff.

Diagram 60

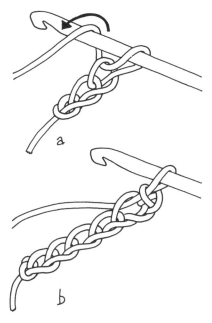

Diagram 61

Chain stitch cord

This is a simple cord which is quick and easy to make. Put a slip knot in the end of your thread (see Diag. 42, p. 39), insert the hook and make a row of chains to the length you want (Diag. 61a).

* Put the hook into the last chain, wrap the yarn round the hook, and pull it through the chain and the loop on the hook* (Diag. 61b). Repeat * to * until the cord is complete. The cord is illustrated on the left of the photograph, showing the reverse side.

Twisted crochet cord

Make a slip knot (see Dig. 42, p. 39) and any number of chains for the length of braid you want (Diag. 61a). Miss 1 chain, *insert the hook into the next chain, wrap the thread round the hook and pull it through the first loop, so that you have 2 loops on the hook (Diag. 62a). Twist the hook horizontally and clockwise one complete turn. Wrap the thread round the hook and pull it through both loops on the hook* (Diag. 62b). Repeat * to * along the chain until the twisted braid is complete (photograph on left).

The next two braids are made using stitches which are used in all kinds of crochet work.

Double crochet (dc) Insert the hook into a chain (ch), wrap the yarn round the hook (yrh) and pull a loop of thread through. Yrh again and pull the yarn through both loops on the hook.

Half treble crochet (htr) Yrh, insert the hook into a chain, yrh again and pull a loop through (3 loops on hook), yrh and pull the thread through all 3 loops.

Treble crochet (tr) Yrh, insert the hook into a chain, yrh again and pull a loop through (3 loops on hook), yrh and pull thread through first 2 loops on hook, yrh and pull through remaining 2 loops.

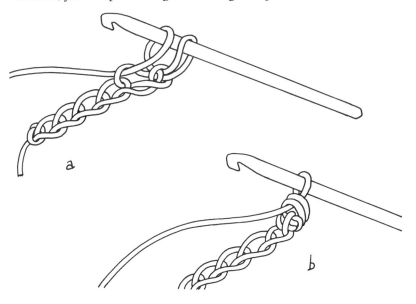

Two crocheted cords, left, chain stitch cord, and right, a twisted crochet cord.

Diagram 62

Double treble crochet (dtr) Yrh twice, insert the hook into a chain, yrh again and pull a loop through (4 loops on hook), (yrh and pull through first 2 loops on hook) twice, yrh and pull through remaining 2 loops.

Braid in two colours

Make 5 ch in A.

Row 1 Make 1 dc into second ch from hook, 1 htr into next ch, 1 tr into next ch. Make 3 dtr into next ch, leaving the last loop of each dtr on the hook. Yrh and pull through all 3 loops on hook. Turn to commence work into chain stitches on one side of pattern.

Row 2 Join in B with a slip knot. *Make 1 dc into first ch st, 1 htr into next ch st, 1 tr into next ch st. Make 3 dtr into next ch st, leaving the last loop of each dtr on the hook. Yrh and pull through all 3 loops on hook. Turn.*

Row 3 Pick up A. Repeat * to *.

Continue by repeating rows 2 and 3 till the braid is the length you want. Keep the colour not in use behind the work, catching it into the crochet stitches so that it doesn't show.

Scalloped braid

Make 8 ch. Join to first ch with a slip stitch, by inserting hook and pulling thread through, to make a circle. Make 3 ch, which count as a first tr. Make 7 tr into the circle, 6 ch, and 1 dc into the circle. Turn the work. *Make 3 ch to count as a first tr, make 7 tr into the 6-ch space, 6 ch, and 1 dc into the 6-ch space, pulling thread so that work closes up in a scallop. Turn the work.* Repeat * to * till the braid is the length you want. A 4-strand cord, see p. 10, has been looped through the chain spaces in the braid illustrated here, to give a more decorative effect.

Two crocheted braids, top, in two colours showing the triangular motifs, and below, a scalloped braid with a 4-strand cord threaded through it.

Woven braids

Silk braid woven with 12 tablets in a double-faced weave. Width 8.5 mm. Excavated from London waterfront deposit and dating from *c*. first half 14th century. Museum of London.

It is uncertain whether the earliest woven braids were a direct development from plaiting fibres and threads, or whether weaving was devised separately in different cultures. There are undoubtedly some close connections between certain plaiting methods and narrow woven braids, particularly in the Peruvian and American Indian finger braids and some traditional Arabic braids. Whatever the case, braid weaving holds a special place in the history of textiles, not only for the beautiful pieces which have been made but also because the weavers have combined great skill with the use of very simple tools.

Woven braids are made using two separate elements; the lengthways threads, or warp, and the crossways thread, or weft, which is passed through the warp to make a woven textile. Whereas in plaiting the threads always travel on a diagonal path to the selvedge, you can recognize a woven braid by the mainly horizontal and vertical interlacing of the threads.

Tablet weaving

Tablet weaving is an ancient method of producing elaborately patterned braids without the need for a frame or loom. The tablets, traditionally made from wood, leather or old playing cards, and nowadays from stiff card or plastic, have been the means of creating some of the most vivid patterns in woven textiles.

The warp is threaded through holes in the tablets and is then stretched taut, either between two fixed points, or attached at one end to a hook or door-handle and by the other to the waist of the weaver. A limitless range of patterns can be made by threading differently coloured warp threads through the tablets which are then rotated in various sequences, and it is these two features which make tablet weaving unique.

The weave structure of tablet-woven braids is warp-faced, meaning that the warp shows on the surface, held closely together by the weft. The particular feature of tablet weaving, however, is that as the tablets are turned, either towards or away from the weaver, the warp twists. Each tablet produces a four-ply twisted rope in the threads. With a number of tablets held side by side, a series of ropes are made, held together by the weft which is passed through the sheds between the upper and lower holes (Diag. 63). It is the combination of differently coloured warp threads, which are brought to the surface of the braid at each turn of the tablets, and the changing angle of the twist in each thread which produces the intricate patterns.

The earliest-known braids date from Ancient Egypt, and there is reference to tablet braids in Ancient Rome from where the skill spread to other parts of Europe. In Scandinavia during the Iron Age quite intricate braids were made as decorative borders to be attached to woven cloth, or as starting borders at the top of the warp on vertical warp-weighted looms. The heyday was in Europe in the Middle Ages when tablet weaving developed from a peasant craft into one which had sophisticated ornamental uses in the church and at court. Fine silk, gold and silver threads were used to make braids to trim vestments and clothing, often with inscriptions and dedications woven in. Tablet weaving still flourishes today, particularly in the Middle and Far East, and in North Africa.

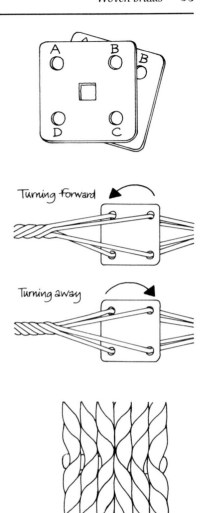

Diagram 63

Materials

The tablets
The equipment needed for tablet weaving is very simple: a set of square, smooth-edged cards with holes at each corner. Tablets can be bought but you can make your own from stiff card, using a sharp paper-cutting knife and a hole-puncher. A set of 30 tablets would be ample to begin with. Depending on the thickness of your warp threads, the more tablets you use, the wider the braid. Cut the tablets about 6 cm ($2\frac{3}{8}$ in.) square, punch holes and label them A, B, C and D clockwise. The lettered side is the front (Diag. 63). Colour the corresponding edges, so that you will see if a tablet is out of order when you are weaving. A square hole in the centre of each tablet will enable you to tie the set up when you pause in the weaving.

The warp and weft
The threads which run the length of the braid make the warp, and they are threaded individually through the holes in the tablets. Because they are held in firm tension during weaving, with the tablets rubbing against them, it is vital you choose strong, smooth threads which won't stretch. A corded or mercerized cotton is ideal to start with; you can weave with wool if it is firmly and evenly spun. As you become more experienced, you may want to try linen or silk which are strong and give a rich and lustrous feel.

In tablet weaving the weft holds the twist in the warp threads in each row and is hardly visible. Use the same colour thread for the weft as the outer warp threads to keep the edges neat. It can be wound into a butterfly (see p. 42) or around a tube of paper small enough to be easily passed through the shed. Ends of weft can be overlapped and joined in the shed.

Other equipment
As well as the tablets and warp and weft threads, these extras will also be helpful: a wooden ruler 30 cm (12 in) long, a pair of G-clamps, a leather belt, strong cord, scissors, a tape measure, a bulldog clip, coloured pens and squared paper.

Thread the yarn from the back
to the front of each tablet

Thread the yarn from the front
to the back of each tablet

Diagram 64

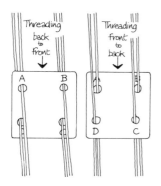

Diagram 65

Pattern drafting and designing

To understand how the patterns in tablet weaving are made and to then be able to design your own, you need to be able to make a pattern chart. As we are concentrating on square tablets with four holes, the chart is four squares deep and labelled to correspond with the holes in the tablets. The numbers along the bottom edge represent each tablet so this chart is for a braid using 12 tablets. The arrows indicate which way to thread each warp thread through the holes in each tablet; threading can be either from back to front or front to back (Diags. 64 and 65).

Method 1

Designing the patterns for tablet-woven braids can be approached in two different ways. In method 1 you can design the weave pattern by drawing symbols in the squares of the chart. Each symbol represents a coloured thread and its position on the chart will tell you which thread to insert through which hole in each tablet, and the threading direction.

The pattern on the chart represents four rows of weaving. If you place a mirror along the bottom edge of the sample chart for method 1, you will see how the pattern can repeat along the braid, in this case to make a diamond. This is woven by turning the tablets four quarter turns towards you, then four quarter turns away repeatedly, and inserting a weft through the shed at each turn, to hold the twist in the warp threads. So with method 1, you can design a variety of different patterns and make them repeat.

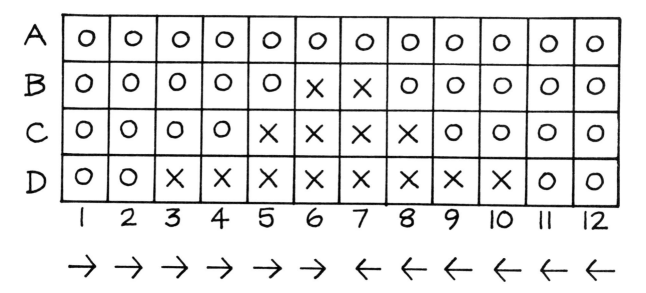

METHOD 1

Method 2

The second method uses a much simpler chart, but the turning sequence is more varied. As the chart for method 2 shows, all the A and B holes are threaded with one colour, and the C and D holes with another which results in a warp with one colour on top and the other below. The scope for designing with this method comes through turning individual tablets in different directions so that the two colours change places. Because the patterns are reversible, this weave is sometimes called double-face.

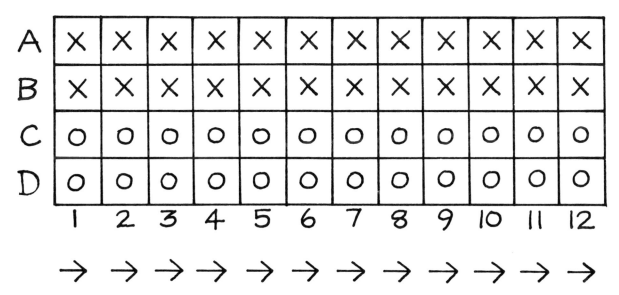

Read through pages 58 to 60 on how to set up tablet weaving, then try a sample braid using method 1 so that you understand how the chart relates to the weave. You could try some variations, see p. 61, or design your own before moving on to try the more complex method 2 braids.

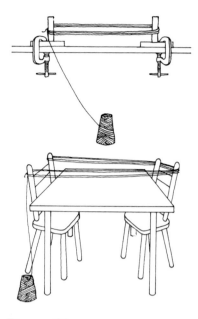

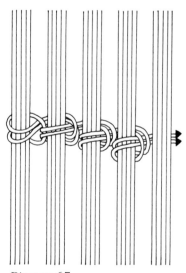

Diagram 66

Diagram 67

Preparing a warp

When calculating the length of your warp, you will need to allow half as much again for take-up during the weaving, so for a braid with a finished length of 3 m (3¼ yards), cut the threads 4.5 m (5 yards) long. Look at the chart you will be working from and add up the total number of threads you will need, for example, in the method 1 chart on p. 56 you would need 34 threads in colour 0 and 14 threads in colour X.

How you wind your warp depends on the length you want; for a short sample braid you can wind directly off your balls of thread and cut them individually. For a long warp this would be impractical, so a more organized system needs to be set up. Whether you use a warping frame, warping posts clamped to a table, two chairs, etc., points A and B need to be the correct distance apart; that is the length of the warp (Diag. 66).

Using the method 1 chart on p.56, start reading from the left at tablet 1. All the holes are colour 0, so tie the end of colour 0 to point A of your warping system. Wind to point B, back to A and then round again, until you have four warp threads. Secure the thread temporarily. You will need to keep these first four threads separate before winding further, so double a separate thread and loop it around the middle of the group. This is the start of a finger chain which will enclose each group of four threads for each tablet within the loops of the chain (Diag. 67). Read the chart at tablet 2. Again, you need four threads in colour 0, so wind again as you did before, finishing at A, and make a loop in the finger chain around this second group. Tablet 3 has three threads in colour 0 for A, B and C holes, but a colour X thread for D hole. Wind your 0 thread three times, then at point B tie colour X to 0, and return to point A with one thread in X. Secure this group in your finger chain. Continue reading each tablet on the chart and, as the threads change colour, knot them to one another at either point A or B, and carry on winding. When all the threads are wound and are secured in the correct order by the chain in the middle, cut them at A and B and lay them flat across a table with the threads for tablet 1 to your left and the ends facing you.

Threading the tablets
Place the pattern chart and tablets on the table and start with the first four warp threads you wound on the left. Thread the correct colours through the holes of the first tablet you pick up. The arrow below tablet 1 will tell you the threading direction. Lay the tablet, lettered face up, on the table. Pick up another tablet and thread the next four warp threads through it according to the chart. Place tablet 2 face up on top of tablet 1 (Diag. 68). Continue in this way, placing each tablet face up on top of the previous one, until you have threaded them all.

Turn the tablets on their sides so that the letters face right with holes A and D uppermost. Tie a ribbon through the centre holes to keep the whole pack secure.

Securing the warp

You can now tie the far ends of the warp together in an overhand knot. Slip a strong cord through it and tie it to a door-knob, a G-clamp fixed to a table or any firm object. If your warp is particularly long and you are working in a limited space, shorten the warp at the far end by chaining it (see p.39).

Remove the chained cord from the middle of the warp, grasp the warp firmly and begin to slide the tablets towards you. Loosen the ribbon a little but take great care not to turn the tablets but to keep them in order and position. You will need to comb out the threads with your fingers as you go, so there are no slack ones, and, as the tablets reach the near end of the warp, all the threads should be evenly tensioned. When you are satisfied they are, trim the ends, and tie them in an overhand knot. Slip a cord through the knot which you will tie to the belt around your waist, but for now, put the warp down carefully till you are ready to weave (Diag. 69).

You will need to get everything prepared so that you can start to weave. If you prefer to sit to weave, position your chair and, next to it, within easy reach, you will need your weft prepared, a ruler to beat the weft in, the chart and a bulldog clip, and you should be wearing a belt around your waist. A little card guide indicating towards and away on either side will help you keep track of your turning sequences. Most important, don't allow yourself to be disturbed by the phone or the doorbell. Tablet weaving is a marvellous and totally absorbing activity to lose yourself in and you will be physically tied up in it too! So set aside a quiet time for this.

Tie the cord holding the near end of the warp to your belt firmly. Position yourself in the chair so that the warp is stretched taut in front of you (Diag. 70). Remember that you are creating the tension in the warp, so sit upright. Untie the cord holding the tablets together, pick up the weft and you are ready to weave.

Diagram 68

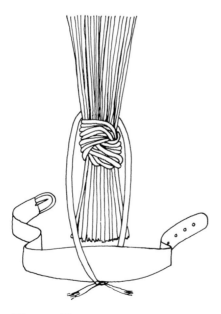

Diagram 69

Weaving braids

There are various turning sequences which can be used in tablet weaving. Let's begin with the basic weaving technique for the simplest braid, i.e. the method 1 braid on p.56.

Turning the tablets four quarter turns each way

1 The starting position has holes A and D uppermost. Pass the weft through the existing shed between the upper and lower threads from right to left, leaving an end of about 10 cm (4 in.). Beat it towards you with the ruler.
2 Take hold of the tablets in both hands and rotate them one quarter turn towards you so that holes A and B are on top. If this seems difficult at first, rotate them individually till you get the hang of it. Slide them up or down the warp a little to separate the threads, making sure threads don't catch on the corners.
3 Put the ruler or the side of your hand between the upper and lower threads to open the new shed, and ease it towards you, checking for stray threads. Pass the weft through from left to right leaving a small loop on the left edge.
4 Turn the tablets another quarter turn so that holes B and C are on the top. Open this shed and pull in the loop of weft so that the threads close up and the edge is neat. Beat towards you, then insert the weft from right to left, leaving a loop on the right edge.
5 Turn the tablets again, so that C and D are on top. Pull in the weft from the last row, beat and insert the weft for this row left to right.
6 Finally turn the tablets so that A and D are on top again. Pull in the loop, beat and insert the weft right to left.

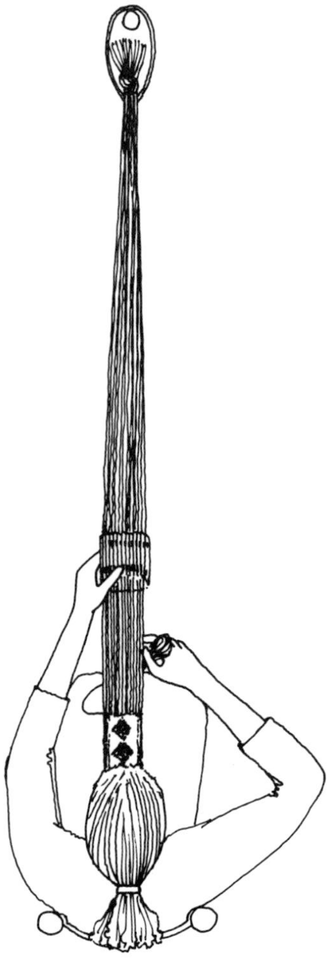

The turning sequence is now reversed by turning the tablets four quarter turns away from you, so that the holes on top will be C and D, B and C, A and B, then A and D again. You will notice that the second turning sequence undoes the twist which built up behind the tablets in the first four turns. Weave the whole braid by alternating the two sequences.

As the weaving progresses, it becomes increasingly difficult to reach the tablets, so you will need to move the braid towards you bit by bit. Undo the cord that is holding the warp to your belt and carefully slide the braid over the belt till the tablets are within easy reach again. Hold the braid in place with a bulldog clip.

Any ends of weft should be overlapped in the shed or darned in afterwards across the braid.

Diagram 70

Variations

When you weave your first braid, you will discover that the design you planned will be bold and clear on one side, with a more broken-angled edge to the patterns on the reverse. The latter are often unexpected and equally attractive, so you have two variations from one chart . You can also create other variations from a chart made as method 1 by changing the turning sequences, so that all kinds of patterns result not only from forward and backward turns of eight, twelve times, etc., but also by re-arranging tablets in the pack. The photo below illustrates this with the original chart.

Here are two braids which use other variations, and from these you can go on to discover the unlimited possibilities of tablet weaving.

Egyptian braid
This braid has a more complex turning sequence, so familiarize yourself fully with method 1 patterns before attempting this. Thread the tablets according to the chart, noting that 1, 2, 17 and 18 are threaded opposite to the rest and so they all face right with holes A and D on top (see p.59). Flip each tablet so that the letters in the top left holes read A, B, C and D, etc., left to right. Number the tablets below the holes 1–18, to help you during weaving. Use a weft in the same colour as the threads in the outer tablets.

Begin by sliding tablets 1–4 up the warp away from you slightly to separate them from the rest. Turn 1–4 towards you, and the rest away. Put the weft in the shed in front of the tablets. Repeat once more. Move two more tablets up the warp from the main pack so that you can turn 1–6 towards you, the rest away. Insert the weft and beat. Repeat. Continue in this way until 1–18 all turn together towards you. Put in the weft, beat and repeat. You can reverse the diagonals by starting on the right with tablets 15–18 turning towards you and the rest away, and continuing to weave until all the tablets are together again.

This braid was threaded according to the chart shown below, and then the tablets were turned in different sequences to create a variety of patterns.

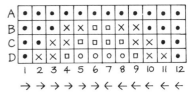

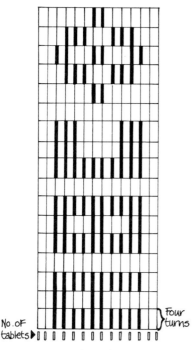

No. of tablets ▶

Four turns

Background = basic turning sequence
Letters = opposite turning sequence

Diagram 71

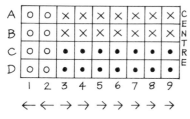

A	o	o	×	×	×	×	×	×	×	C
B	o	o	×	×	×	×	×	×	×	E
C	o	o	•	•	•	•	•	•	•	N T R
D	o	o	•	•	•	•	•	•	•	E

    1   2   3   4   5   6   7   8   9

← ← → → → → → → →

The chart shown here was the threading arrangement for both the Egyptian braid, top, and the double-faced lettered braid, below.

Double-face braid

With the double-face technique you can weave letters, figures and motifs which appear in one colour on top and come out in reverse underneath the braid. At first you will need all your concentration but, once you have mastered this, it opens up a lot of scope for designing.

Use the same chart as for the Egyptian braid but, before you begin to weave, flip the tablets so that A and B are on top, bringing one colour to the top of the warp and the other below. You are now already in the first step of the basic turning sequence which is as follows: turn the tablets away so that A and B are on top. Turn them away so that D and A are on top. Turn them towards you so that A and B are on top. Turn them towards you so that B and C are on top. These four turns will make a plain braid with one colour above and the other underneath.

To make letters or motifs, the tablets have to be separated into two groups. For the **background** colour, slide tablets up the warp and turn them in **the basic sequence**. For **letters and motifs** slide tablets down the warp and turn them in **the opposite way to the basic sequence** so that the colour underneath is brought to the top to contrast with the background colour. The colours in the patterns will be reversed on top and underneath. Each turn of the two groups is made simultaneously and the weft is passed through the shed in front of all tablets. A chart showing how to turn tablets in either direction to make shapes is very helpful and an example of how this can be done is shown in Diag. 71.

Backstrap weaving

Backstrap weaving is a method of producing braids and narrow lengths of cloth on a simple portable loom. It is a technique which has been widely used all over the world, from the Far East to South America, and is still carried on in some areas today. The main parts of the loom are simplicity itself; two sticks or beams between which the warp threads are stretched, a tying cord which holds the back stick to a post or door-handle and, at the near end of the warp, attached to the front stick, a backstrap which can be either a piece of leather or a woven band, which is worn around the waist or hips of the weaver and from which the loom takes its name. During the weaving it is the body of the weaver, sitting or standing upright, which controls the tension of the warp and is an integral part of the loom. In addition, a means of opening sheds in the warp has to be created so that the weft can be passed through to make the weave. This is done with two sticks held in the warp. One is known as a rod and the other as a heddle stick. They are used alternately throughout the weaving.

If you are interested in traditional methods of weaving braids, then the backstrap loom will fascinate you and it has many advantages. It is easily assembled from simple materials, is portable and can be set up almost anywhere and rolled up and put away when not in use. It is for these reasons that backstrap weaving has endured throughout history and, as one of the first looms invented, has been used in different forms in India, Japan, Indonesia and Africa as well as Central and South America, where in Mexico, Peru, Bolivia and Guatemala the tradition continues of weaving narrow strips to make and decorate regional clothing.

Indian women backstrap weaving in Mexico City. Photograph by J. Foreman.

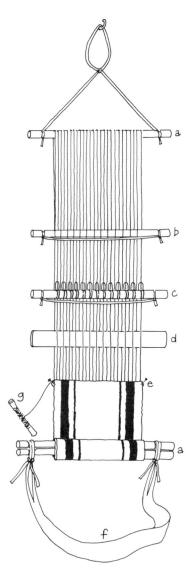

Diagram 72

Materials

The backstrap loom

Most backstrap looms have the following parts in common as shown in Diag. 72. The back and front sticks, called beams (a), support the warp with an additional beam used at the front to roll the weaving around. Two more sticks are attached to the warp to make the alternate sheds for plain weaving. The rod (b) makes the stick shed and the heddle stick (c), with cotton loops attached to it and the warp, makes the pull shed. Another flat stick, the batten or beater (d), holds the shed open so that the weft can be passed through and also beats it down. A width gauge or stretcher (e) is pinned to the back of the weaving to help maintain an even width. An emery board will do very well. The backstrap (f) holds the front beam to the weaver and can be a strip of leather or you can weave one as a project. The weft (g), wound round a tube of paper, is woven through the warp. Finally a very strong cord with a centre loop is used to attach the back beam to a post or door-handle.

To make a backstrap loom which will allow you to weave up to 7.5 cm (3 in.) wide braids, cut your sticks 15 cm (6 in.) long. For wider braids cut the sticks proportionately longer. You will need 5 round sticks made from 1.25 cm ($\frac{1}{2}$ in.) wooden dowel and 1 flat stick made from 2 cm × 5 mm ($\frac{3}{4}$ × $\frac{1}{4}$ in.) wooden baton. Cut grooves at each end of the dowels about 2.5 cm (1 in.) from the ends. Sandpaper all the sticks till they are smooth.

The warp and weft

Like tablet weaving, the warp threads which run the length of the braid are held in very firm tension so they have to be strong and smooth. Use a medium weight corded or mercerized cotton for your first braids, then graduate to silk or wool, which must be tightly spun. Rub beeswax on the warp threads to prevent fluff building up on the cotton heddles which are constantly rubbing against the warp. Wax the cotton for the heddles as well. Backstrap braids are warp faced, with the warp visible on the surface and held closely together by the weft which doesn't show. Use the same type and colour thread for the weft as the outermost warp threads. For pick-up and striped braids, use the same type of thread throughout, but you could vary the thickness slightly and contrast matt with shiny threads for interesting texture.

Other equipment

You will also need a pair of G-clamps and two warping posts. These can easily be made. Cut two 13 cm (5 in.) lengths of 2 cm ($\frac{3}{4}$ in.) wooden dowel and two pieces of wood about 7.5 cm (3 in.) square by 2 cm ($\frac{3}{4}$ in.) thick. Drill a hole through the centre of each piece of wood and also a little way into each dowel at one end. Glue and screw the dowel into the bases with 5 cm (2 in.) screws (Diag. 73).

Colour plate: Backstrap woven braids, l to r: (1) pick-up patterned braid being worked on a backstrap loom, (2 & 3) braids with pick-up patterns, and (4) with warp-faced striped patterns.

Setting up a backstrap loom

Winding the warp

To calculate the length of the warp you will need, refer to p. 58 on preparing the warp. Winding the warp for a backstrap loom differs from the tablet-weaving method, because you wind in a figure of eight around two fixed points to make a cross in the warp. This will keep the alternate threads in their correct order and enable you to insert a rod in one group and make heddles with the other for the sheds. Clamp the warping posts to the edge of a table the required distance apart. To wind the warp, tie the end to one post and wind the thread continuously around both posts in a figure of eight (Diag. 73). A complete turn around both posts will give you two warp ends and for a first sample braid 20 ends would be sufficient. Make sure the tension of the warp is even and that the last threads aren't tighter than the first. An uneven warp is very difficult to weave. Tie the final end to the post and also tie two threads loosely through the warp either side of the cross at the centre.

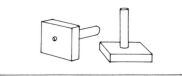

Your warp can be in one colour or you can make beautiful warp-striped backstrap braids by warping different coloured threads together. This is done by knotting the different threads to one another at the posts (not **to** the posts) as you wind the warp. Alternating coloured threads at every half round, so that you change colour at each post, will give a horizontal stripe when you weave. One colour shows in one row, the other in the next. Two coloured threads surrounded by a contrasting colour will give the thinnest vertical stripe you can weave, so you can change the colours as you wind to create varied widths of stripes. I have included some samples on p. 68.

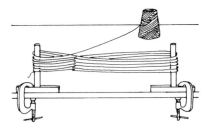

Diagram 73

Tying the warp to the loom

Take two of the round sticks as the front and back beams of the loom and slip each one down alongside the posts at either ends of the warp. Carefully ease the warp off the posts and onto the beams and gently lay it flat on the table. Attach the tying cord to the back beam with a loop centred exactly in the middle and hook it to a post or door-handle, with the warp laid out carefully. If your warp is very long and your space is limited, roll the warp around the back beam and an extra stick to shorten it, see p. 64.

You will now need to gather everything around you before you attach the front beam to your waist. Position your chair if you are going to sit (an upright wooden chair is best) and place the other sticks, the weft, a tying cord, smooth waxed cotton for heddles, scissors and paper within easy reach. Put the backstrap round your waist, pick up the warp and using a strong tying cord, attach the front beam to the backstrap. Adjust your position so the warp is stretched out in front of you in the same way as in tablet weaving (see Diag. 70).

Colour plate: Assortment of tassels using silk, rayon, leather, metallic threads, feathers and beads.

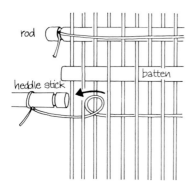

Diagram 74

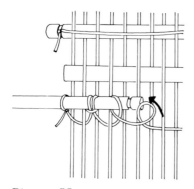

Diagram 75

Inserting the rod and making the heddles

The two sticks needed to make the sheds for plain weaving are now inserted into the warp; one round stick or rod is inserted for the stick shed, the other has cotton loops or heddles attached to it and the alternate warp threads for the pull shed.

First pass one stick, now called the rod, through the warp where the far cross-tie is. Remove the cross-tie. Tie a thread from one end of the rod to the other, in the grooves, to prevent it from falling out.

Now pull up the other cross-tie and pass the flat stick (the batten), through in the same place. Remove this cross-tie. Pass one end of your waxed cotton through this shed from right to left. Tie a loop in the end and slip it over the end of the other round stick, now called the heddle stick. Hold the heddle stick in your left hand and with your right hand pull up a loop in the cotton between the first and second warp threads lying above the batten. Twist the loop anti-clockwise and slip it on to the stick (Diag. 73). Make another loop in the same place, clockwise this time, and slip it on to the stick. The depth of your heddles should be about 3 cm ($1\frac{1}{4}$ in.). Make a second heddle by pulling on the cotton between the second and third warp threads above the batten, and continue in this way across the warp to the last thread (Diag. 75). Tie the end of cotton to the beginning across the heddle stick.

Weaving braids

Wind the weft on to a tube of paper or make a butterfly (see p. 42). Push all the warp threads close together and sit upright so that you maintain the tension of the warp. If you want a fringe at the beginning, insert a strip of paper into the warp to allow for this. Plain weaving consists of two rows which are repeated alternately.

Row 1 Push the rod up the warp out of the way. Lift the heddle stick so that it opens the first shed, called the pull shed (Diag. 76). This will be made easier if at the same time you hold the batten in your other hand and flick the end across the warp immediately behind and then in front of the heddle stick, until the upper and lower threads separate. Put the batten in the shed, turn it on end, and pass the weft through from right to left, leaving a short end. Beat the weft towards you.

Row 2 Bring the rod down the warp towards you until it is immediately behind the heddle stick, so that the shed for this row opens in front of the heddles. This is the stick shed. Flick the batten across the warp in front of the heddles to help the threads separate. Put the batten in the shed, turn it on end and pass the weft from left to right, leaving a small loop at the left edge. Tuck the weft end in this row and beat the weft towards you (Diag. 77).

   Continue weaving these two rows alternately, drawing in the loop from the previous row so that the warp threads close up, and beating the weft towards you. Any ends can be overlapped in the sheds. When it becomes difficult to reach the shed sticks, untie the warp from your backstrap and put your extra stick on top of the weaving next to the front beam. Roll up the weaving and retie your backstrap to the ends of the extra stick. Weave the braid to the length you want, leave a fringe allowance at the far end, then cut the warp from the front and back beams. Finish with fringes or tassels (see p. 71).

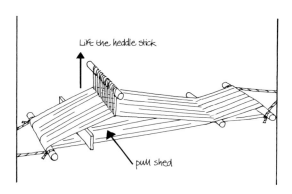

Diagram 76

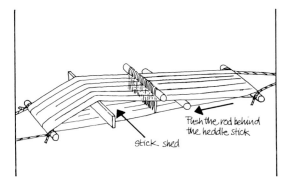

Diagram 77

Charts 1, 2 and 3 correspond with
the three warp-faced striped braids
shown here left to right.

Warp-faced striped patterns

If you wind different coloured threads in the warp, you can weave all kinds
of patterned braids with vertical and horizontal stripes. I have included
some simple pattern charts with the corresponding weaves here for you to
begin with. Each square represents one warp end and you read the chart
from left to right, winding the warp according to the colour indicated.
Arrange the colours as described on p. 65. The width of braids is decided by
the thickness and number of threads used, so you could develop these ideas
into more intricate braids by using more threads and colours and varying
the thickness and texture of threads. The braid in the photograph facing
p. 64 is in fine mercerized cotton and is 3 cm ($1\frac{1}{4}$ in.) wide with 67 warp
ends.

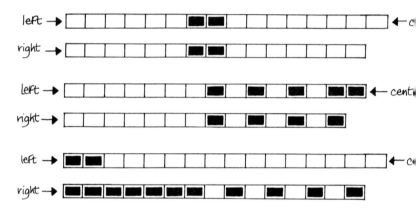

Pick-up patterns

Another way of making patterns involves picking up warp threads with
the fingers from the back warp layer to the surface to create geometric
patterns and motifs. This requires a lot of concentration but the results are
exciting and well worth the effort. Do not attempt pick-ups till you have
mastered plain weaving.

   You can weave these braids either on a backstrap loom or you may find
it easier on a frame with suspended rods as described on p. 23. Either way,
the warp should be wound around the warping posts or rods of the frame,
but not in a figure of eight. The warp arrangement for pick-up braids has
two colours alternating in the centre pick-up area with border stripes
either side. Follow the chart for a first sample braid and, when you come to
the alternating colours in the centre, wind all the threads for one colour
first and temporarily secure the end. Then wind the other colour between
each thread of the first colour and tie this end to that of the other colour.
This saves you from having to cut and tie ends at each end of the warp.
You now need to find the two sheds in the warp for weaving. On the frame
the warp is already flat but, if you are backstrap weaving, transfer the
warp on to the front and back beams as described on p. 66; then attach
tying cords to each beam and loop them over the posts so that the warp is
stretched out again but flat. You can now sit beside the warp to make the
sheds.

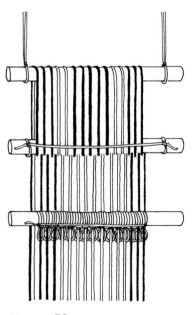

Diagram 78

Near the top of the warp use a knitting needle to pick up every other thread, so that in the centre area all the black threads are on top. Don't worry too much about order of threads above it, some may have to twist. Insert the rod into this shed and tie a cord around it to make it secure. Take out the needle and, working below the rod, now pick up every thread which lies behind the rod. Make heddles for this shed as described on p. 66 and in Diag. 78. Ease the sheds down the warp to the beginning. Insert a strip of paper for fringe allowance and you are ready to weave.

Plain weave for a few rows. This will make a pattern of black and white horizontal stripes in the centre pattern area. Now try a pick-up pattern, say the first triangle shown in the design below (Diag. 79). Each vertical bar represents one white picked-up thread.

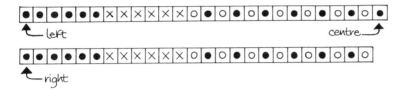

Start in the stick shed with the black threads on top in the centre area. Find the centre white thread below. Pick it up so it lies with the black threads. Pass the weft through this shed. Weave a plain row in the pull shed. In the next stick shed, pick up the two white threads either side of the previous one. Pass the weft through, then weave another plain row in the pull shed. Continue in this way so that on each pick-up row you pick up more alternate white threads to shape the triangle.

Continue to follow the designs below for more motifs, then try designing your own or extend the idea to weave lettering and figures.

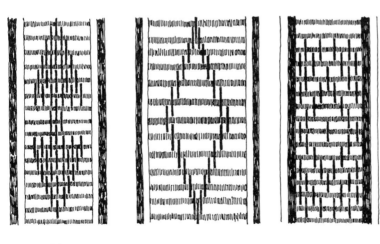

Diagram 79

The chart corresponds with the woven braid illustrated here, with patterns using the pick-up technique.

A Victorian tassel made around a mould.

Fringes, tassels and finishing techniques

All kinds of fringes, tassels and finishes can be used to embellish textiles, some as part of the work itself, some as additional decoration. Whichever textile you are interested in, I hope you will find the techniques described here of interest to you and will possibly no longer need to search through haberdashery departments to find a particular cord, fringed trimming or tassel when you are able to make your own in exactly the colour and thread of your choice, to complement your piece of work.

First I will describe some finishing techniques suitable for braids described earlier in the book, and then go on to ways of making fringes and tassels, a number of which use techniques such as plaiting, knotting and weaving referred to in earlier chapters.

Finishing braids

Ending with a straight edge
This applies mainly to plaited braids, where the threads travel on a diagonal path. In most cases, the ends of the braids finish with slanting edges which may be desirable, but you may sometimes prefer to finish with a straight horizontal edge, before making decorative fringes. Plaiting or weaving to a straight edge needs to begin as you approach the ends. The weft threads which come from the shorter edge of the braid should stop one warp thread short in each successive row, so that when all the weft threads have been passed through the warp threads, the finished edges are horizontal (Diag. 80).

Philippine edge
This edging is made with a series of half-hitches (see p. 43). Start with the third thread from the left. Make a half-hitch with it by passing it to the left, over the first and second threads, then round behind them, and pull the end through (Diag. 80). Pull tight. Let the third thread drop down with the rest again. Make another half-hitch with the fourth thread, looping it round the second and third threads. Continue with all the threads in turn. Several rows make an attractive herringbone edge to the braid.

Finishing with overhand knots
One of the simplest methods of securing the ends of threads is to tie overhand knots in them (see p. 9). Two or more threads can be included in a series of knots or a whole group can be knotted together in one large knot.

There are many more ways of finishing braids, and of dealing with the
ends of threads in other textile crafts, either to give a secure and decorative
finish, or to add an edging to complete the piece of work. I have included a
range of methods for you to dip into in the next section on fringes.

Ending with a straight edge

Fringes

A fringe is an edging or border which can enhance a piece of textile work,
either by using the existing threads in the piece, or by making a separate
border which can be added with stitches, knots or crochet. I have differen-
tiated the fringes here by the technique used to make them.

Plaited
Any of the plaits described in the first part of the plaiting chapter, where
the ends of the threads are free, can be used to make attractive fringes.
When you are making a plaited fringe on a braid, allow a good length of
threads, say at least 15 cm (6 in.) to allow for take up in the plaiting, and so
that the fringe won't look skimped. The ends of the plaits can be secured
with overhand knots (see p. 9) or wrapping (see p. 73) to prevent them
from unravelling (Diag. 80).

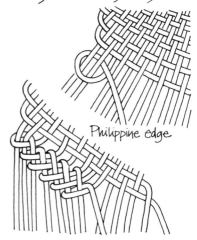

Philippine edge

Corded
A number of the round plaits in the plaiting chapter can be used to make
corded fringes. Making a twisted cord is another simple alternative. Allow
half as much again to the length of the threads for the finished fringe.
Cords are made with several threads twisted together, a group of four, for
example, or with a thread which is doubled and twisted from the centre.
Pin each thread to a board, or weight it down, at the top end. Hold one
thread taut at the near end and twist it tightly till it begins to spiral on itself
if you slacken it off. If you are using plied threads, twist in the same
direction as the ply. Pin or weight the twisted thread down temporarily.
Repeat with the other threads. Now take hold of them all, and twist them
in the opposite direction, to make the cord. Secure the ends with a knot or
wrapping (Diag. 80). Cords made in two or more colours like this make a
spiral pattern.

Plaited and corded fringes

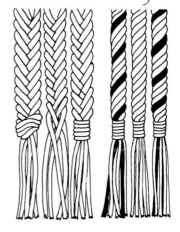

Knotted
As well as overhand knots more elaborate macramé fringes can be made,
either using the existing ends of a fairly wide braid or textile, or by
attaching extra threads to the fabric, or by making a fringe on a holding
cord, which can be stitched on as a border.
　Macramé in fact derives from an Arabic word meaning fringe and in the
Victorian era, when it was fashionable to have interiors which were rich in
decoration, all manner of very elaborate fringes and trimmings were made
from a combination of macramé knots. In the chapter on knotted braids, I
have described how to make a variety of knots, and you can use them as
the basis for fringes and edgings, adding tassels and beads for an even
richer effect. In the same way as making knotted braids, you will need a
soft board or a firm cushion and pins to carry out the work and you will
need to allow enough length for the finished fringe (see p.41).

Diagram 80

Macramé fringe with horizontal
and diagonal clove hitches

Here are just a few ideas you may like to try, and which might help you to develop your own. Smooth, fairly firm threads suit macramé fringing best, such as cotton, silk, and some shiny synthetics. Adding tassels (see p. 74) gives weight and fullness to fringes and finishes them off well.

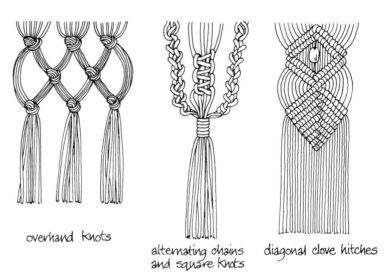

overhand knots   alternating chains   diagonal clove hitches
                        and square knots

Diagram 82

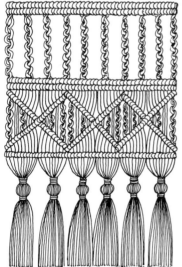

with horizontal and diagonal hitches,
alternating chains and tassels

Diagram 81

Woven and crocheted

Tablet-woven braids which combine the rich patterns in the weave and the use of threads like silk or linen can make very decorative braids with fringes.

Set the warp up as described on p. 58. Cut a strip of card as wide as you want the fringe to be. The weft is passed through the shed and around the card alongside the warp, then back into the next shed and so on. The fringe can be cut or left as loops, and you can thread beads on to it or add tassels.

Fringes can also be made with a crochet heading. The fringe illustrated here was made as follows. The dark thread is a doubled length which acts as a foundation for the fringe and the crochet. Put the centre of the dark thread on the hook, then a slip knot of the light thread. Make 6 dc (see p. 53) in light thread around the dark thread. Turn and make a 2nd row of 6 dc into the 1st row, inserting the hook into the two loops of each stitch below and working over the dark double thread as well. Wrap the double thread round a strip of card 5 cm (2 in.) wide to make the first fringe loop, then secure it with a chain in the light thread. Work a row of 6 dc into the previous row. Work 6 dc round the double thread. (This is repeated every 4th row.) Turn. Work 6 dc into the previous row. Make another loop as before and continue. Double twist each loop to make cords (see p. 71) and add tassels (see p. 74). Stitch into the crochet heading with black thread.

Wrapping

Wrapping is a method of binding one thread around a core or foundation, in this case, a group of threads. To be successful, the core must be thicker than the wrapping thread, the ends of which must be securely fastened inside the wrapping itself. I have included various ways in which wrapping can be used in the illustrations on these pages.

Start by laying one end of the wrapping thread parallel with the core of threads. Working from the top downwards, wrap firmly round the core, trapping the end inside. As the wrapping approaches the length you want, lay a loop of thin strong thread over the wrapping. Continue binding with the wrapping thread, enclosing the looped thread inside. Pass the finishing end of the wrapping thread through the loop. Pull the loop up, bringing the end inside the wrapping. Trim the end close to the wrapping (Diag. 83 a–e).

If you want to wrap with a series of different types or colours of threads, one after the other, lay the finishing end of one colour parallel with the core, then start as you did at the beginning with a new thread, wrapping it around the core, and trapping the two ends inside.

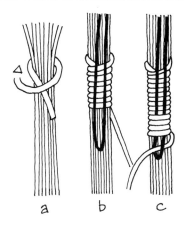

a   b   c

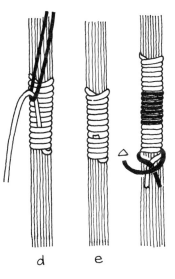

d   e

Diagram 83

Left: a tablet woven fringe in which the weft was extended on one edge to make a fringe. Right: a crochet heading holds the dark foundation thread which was then made into a corded fringe to hold the tassels.

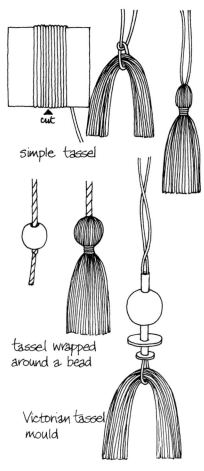

simple tassel

tassel wrapped
around a bead

Victorian tassel
mould

Diagram 84

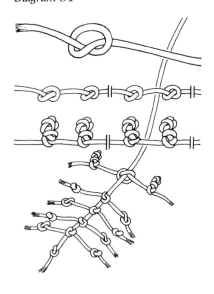

Diagram 85

Tassels

Adding tassels to braids and to the edges and corners of textiles adds weight and fullness as well as making a very decorative finish. Most types of thread which hang well are suitable, particularly smooth cottons, silks and shiny synthetics. Combine them with fringes, plaits and cords to give a luxurious effect.

Simple tassel

The simplest tassel is made by first wrapping thread around a piece of stiff card to the length and fullness you require. Cut the threads along the bottom edge and secure them in the middle with a knot of the same thread or a loop to hang the tassel by. The tassel is them completed with wrapping, a little way down from the top, (Diag. 84). A fuller head can be made on the tassel by using a round bead with a hole through it, which first has a cord threaded through it to hold the tassel. Arrange a number of cut threads around the bead, sufficient to cover it completely, then add a wrapped thread just below the bead. The ends of the tassel are finally trimmed to the length you want (Diag. 84).

Victorian tassels were often quite large, and richly ornamented with additional cords and braids stitched on, crochet work made over the top of the basic tassel, and even multi-tasselled with layers of smaller tassels added, and hanging down from the head. They were used as furnishing trimmings, for curtains, tie-backs, bell-pulls, etc., and were made on a wooden mould like the one illustrated here. It shows a hollow wooden bar slotted through two round discs below a wooden ball. A cord through the centre holds the base tassel, and the main tassel is made as described above. The photograph on p. 70 illustrates a Victorian tassel made in this way and richly decorated.

Knotted tassel

This unusual tassel is made from threads with overhand knots tied on them, which are then cut and knotted on to a supporting cord. Shiny soft threads which fray at the ends are effective. The knots are single small ones and large double ones. Make the small knots by tying overhand knots in a single thread, at least 3.5 cm ($1\frac{3}{8}$ in.) apart. (The distance should allow for a further knot to tie it on to the supporting cord and will vary depending on the thickness of thread you are using.) Cut between pairs of knots till you have twelve in all. Make the large knots by tying four together, at least 4.5 cm ($1\frac{1}{2}$ in.) apart, and cut between pairs, to make six in all (Diag. 85). Make a cord with a doubled thread, pinning it down at the centre loop and double twisting it (see p. 71). Hold the twist with an overhand knot at the ends. Attach the small knots to the cord with overhand knots, then the large ones (Diag. 85). Trim the ends close to the knots. Slide them down the cord till they are close together and secure them with a single knot on the cord. Tassels like this can be multi-coloured or more small knotted tassel groups can be added further up the supporting cord (photograph facing p. 65).

Pompom

Pompoms bring back childhood memories of mittens and woolly hats. They look quite different made in various sizes in shiny cotton, silk or linen, held by twisted cords to the ends of braids or edges of textiles, especially when combined with fringing.

Cut two circles of card, the size you want your tassel to be. Make a hole in the centre of both. Thread a good length of doubled thread on to a large-eyed needle and wind the thread tightly and closely round the two circles held together. Trap the beginning end into the outer edge of the binding, and any other ends from more lengths of thread if needed. Cut the thread carefully around the outer edge of the circle and gradually ease the two card circles apart a little. Make a twisted cord (see p. 71) to hold the pompom with one thread doubled and twisted from the loop. Tie an over-hand knot a little way from the ends, then wrap the ends around the centre of the pompom. Tie them tightly (Diag. 86). Cut into each card circle and ease them off the pompom.

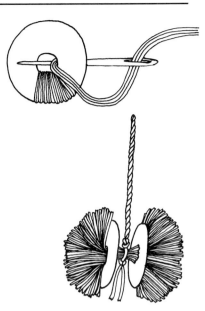

Diagram 86

Left, a simple tassel made by wrapping threads over a bead, centre, a knotted tassel, and right, a pompom.

GLOSSARY

Balanced weave   the warp and weft are interwoven so both show equally in the weave

Braid   a narrow textile which is made using various techniques such as plaiting, knotting, weaving, etc.

Butterfly   a small bundle of yarn wound in a figure of eight so that the end may be pulled out when needed

Chaining   made with a continuous thread in which each consecutive loop is pulled through the previous one to form a braid

Interlacing   a flat over-and-under method of connecting threads, as in the Hopi wedding sash and finger-woven braids

Interlinking   in which one part of a continuous thread is connected with another part by a twist, to make an elastic, netlike textile, as in sprang

Interlocking   in which one thread is twisted around another to connect them, as in the finger-woven American Indian lightning pattern

Knotting   threads are looped round and through one another and pulled into knots to hold the structure firm, either in a continuous thread, or separate threads as in macramé

Looping   in which a continuous thread is turned back on itself to form a loop through which another part, or the end, of the thread may pass, as in knitting, netting and crochet

Macramé   a descriptive term, adopted in the nineteenth century, for the craft of tying fancy knots with several separate threads

Plaiting   separate threads which are interlaced on a diagonal path in a systematic way

Repp   an ancient Peruvian technique used in finger weaving in which grouped wefts are woven through single warps, or single wefts are woven through grouped warps

Sinnet or sennit   a narrow braid made from the same knot repeated continuously

Sprang   in which threads are stretched and secured at both ends and twisted around one another to produce a netlike textile

Twining   in which pairs of threads are twisted around one another so one pair encloses another; in twined plaiting, the twining takes opposite diagonal paths

Warp   the lengthways threads through which the crossways or weft threads are passed

Warp ends   individual warp threads

Warp-faced weave   the warp ends are pulled closely together and held by the weft so that only the warp shows on the surface

Weaving   consists of two separate sets of threads; the warp, or lengthways threads, held in tension, through which the weft, or crossways threads are passed

Weft   the thread or threads, woven through the warp crossways to form the weaving

Weft-faced weave   the weft is beaten down firmly in a highly tensioned warp, so only the weft shows on the surface

LIST OF SUPPLIERS

United Kingdom

Barnhowe Spinning and Woodturning
Elterwater
Ambleside
Cumbria LA22 9HW

Dryad
PO Box 38
Northgates
Leicester LE1 9BU

Fibrecrafts
Style Cottage
Lower Eashing
Godalming
Surrey GU7 2QD

The Handweavers Studio and Gallery
29 Haroldstone Road
London E17 7AN

Texere Yarns
College Mill
Barkerend Road
Bradford BD3 9AQ

North America

Cotton Clouds
RR #2, Desert Hills 16
Safford, AZ 85446
USA

Frederick Fawcett
1304 Scott Street
Petaluma, CA 94952
USA

Cheryl Kolander
5806 North Vancouver
Portland, OR 97217
USA

The Silk Tree
Box 78
Whonnock, BC
Canada VOM 1SO

BIBLIOGRAPHY

Backstrap Weaving   Barbara Taber and Marilyn Anderson, Watson-Guptill (1975)

Band Weaving   Harold and Sylvia Tacker, Studio Vista (1975)

The Basic Book of Fingerweaving   Esther Warner Dendel, Nelson (1975)

Beyond Weaving   Marcia Chamberlain and Candace Crockett, Watson-Guptill/Pitman (1974)

Card Weaving   Candace Crockett, Watson-Guptill (1973)

Encyclopaedia of Needlework   Therese de Dillmont, DMC Library (nd)

Finger Weaving, Indian Braiding   Alta Turner, Sterling Publishing Co. & Oak Tree Press 3rd edn (1977)

Making Plaits and Braids   June Barker, Batsford (1973)

The Manual of Braidmaking   Noemi Speiser, published by author, Basel, Switzerland (1983)

The Primary Structure of Fabrics   Irene Emery, Textile Museum, Washington, rev. edn (1980)

Tablet Weaving   Ann Sutton and Pat Holtom, Batsford (1975)

The Techniques of Sprang   Peter Collingwood, Faber & Faber (1974)

The Techniques of Tablet Weaving   Peter Collingwood, Faber & Faber (1982)

Textile and Weaving Structures   Peter Collingwood, Batsford (1987)

The Weaving, Spinning and Dyeing Book   Rachel Brown, Routledge & Kegan Paul (1979)

INDEX